God in the Tumult of the Global Square

God in the Tumult of the Global Square

RELIGION IN GLOBAL CIVIL SOCIETY

Mark Juergensmeyer,
Dinah Griego, and John Soboslai

UNIVERSITY OF CALIFORNIA PRESS

University of California Press, one of the most distinguished university presses in the United States, enriches lives around the world by advancing scholarship in the humanities, social sciences, and natural sciences. Its activities are supported by the UC Press Foundation and by philanthropic contributions from individuals and institutions. For more information, visit www.ucpress.edu.

University of California Press
Oakland, California

Library of Congress Cataloging-in-Publication Data

Juergensmeyer, Mark, author.
    God in the tumult of the global square : religion in global civil society / Mark Juergensmeyer, Dinah Griego, and John Soboslai.
        p.   cm.
    Includes bibliographical references and index.
    ISBN 978-0-520-28346-6 (cloth, alk. paper) — ISBN 978-0-520-28347-3 (pbk., alk. paper) — ISBN 978-0-520-95932-3 (electronic)
    1. Religion and civil society.   2. Religion and sociology.   3. Religion and politics.   4. Globalization—Religious aspects.   I. Griego, Dinah, author.   II. Soboslai, John, author.   III. Title.
BL65.C62J84   2015
201'.7—dc23   2015001143

Manufactured in the United States of America

24   23   22   21   20   19   18   17   16   15
10   9   8   7   6   5   4   3   2   1

In keeping with a commitment to support environmentally responsible and sustainable printing practices, UC Press has printed this book on Natures Natural, a fiber that contains 30% post-consumer waste and meets the minimum requirements of ANSI/NISO Z39.48-1992 (R 1997) (*Permanence of Paper*).

To the memory of Robert Bellah

CONTENTS

For introductory videos to each chapter, go to ucpress.edu/go/globalsquare.

ACKNOWLEDGMENTS

The roots of the project on which this book is based, "Religion in Global Civil Society," go back to 2008, when the Henry Luce Foundation provided seed money for an exploratory workshop on the topic. A group of scholars and representatives of international humanitarian organizations in different parts of the world came together in Santa Barbara for a one-day meeting to assess how religion is changing in the global era and how these changes affect the work of civil society groups and movements. Inevitably, the discussion broadened to include the whole range of social changes in the global era and the role of religion in public life. It was a thoughtful occasion, one full of fertile ideas.

The success of that workshop soon led to a proposal for an extended project to last from 2010 to 2014, for which the Luce Foundation provided the major funding, as part of their initiative on religion in international affairs. Our thanks to everyone in the foundation who has persevered and supported our efforts over the years, including Michael Gilligan, Toby Volkman, and Terry Lautz—who first encouraged us to develop this idea into a sustained project.

The project was hosted by the Orfalea Center for Global and International Studies at the University of California, and our thanks to staff and faculty related to the Center. Since the director of the center at the time, Mark Juergensmeyer, was the principal investigator of the project and one of the authors of this book, there is no need (and maybe no reason) to thank him. But we do appreciate the constant support of the program director, Victor Faessel—the director's right hand man—who attended all of the workshops and was an active member of the project team. The coordinator of the Luce project, who made the arrangements and held the whole thing together, was

Dinah Griego, who is a coauthor of this book. Regina Rivera was our webmaster and publications czar, who artfully designed the project's website and printed reports from each of the workshops. Oversight of the budget, payments, and other financial matters were provided by the center's office manager, Cori Montgomery, and by her worthy replacement, Kim Coonen.

The discussions in each of the workshops were transcribed and summaries created for the workshop reports and to serve as background for this book. For this reason we relied on a small army of graduate student writers, including a master wordsmith, John Soboslai, who is a coauthor of this book. Among the other writers were John Ucciferri, Sara Kamali, Linda Khoury, Mayumi Kodani, Vikas Malhotra, Aleksandra Malinowska, Erica Mesker, Barbara Morra, Nicolas Pascal, Sergey Saluschev, Aaron Sokoll, Michael Starks, and Aisa Villanueva. The chief videographer for the project was Paul Lynch, who filmed most of the footage that can be seen on the project's website and that is embedded within the e-book version of this book. Lynch also created the short video introductions for each chapter and the half-hour video program that summarizes the book as a whole. The full archive of videos related to the project can be found at www.orfaleacenter.ucsb.edu/luce.

Many of our colleagues at Santa Barbara were involved in the planning for the project or participated in the workshops. Several research fellows of the center, notably Richard Falk, Hilal Elver, Mona Sheikh, Manoranjan Mohanty, and Bidyut Mohanty, were actively involved in multiple sessions. Faculty in the UCSB global studies program who participated included Giles Gunn, Eve Darian-Smith, Phil McCarty, Jan Nederveen Pieterse, Nadege Clitandre, Aashish Mehta, and Paul Amar. Religious studies colleagues included Wade Clark Roof, Kathleen Moore, Gurinder Singh Mann, Juan Campo, and Magda Campo. Other UCSB faculty contributing were Nancy Gallagher, Kathleen Bruhn, John Foran, Kum Kum Bhavnani, Gurinder Singh Mann, Sarah Cline, and Claudine Michel.

At the heart of the project were a series of workshops, most of which were held at Santa Barbara. These included the initial planning workshop, a networking workshop at the beginning of the project, a capstone workshop at the end, and three region-focused workshops: Latin America and Caribbean, South and Southeast Asia, and Africa and the Middle East. Our thanks to the many student assistants who helped make these Santa Barbara workshops a success, including Anila Arif, Cory Baker, Peter Boraas, Nick Cook, Collin Dvorak, Brad Greenbaum, Amanda Maxi, Kendra Sarna, and Eva Van Wingerden.

Five of the workshops were held abroad, and in each case we relied on cosponsors in these locales. In Buenos Aires, the workshop was cosponsored with Universidad del Cema. Our cohosts were Carlos Escude, who was director of the Centro de Estudios Internacionales y de Educacion para la Globalizacion (CEIEG); and Fernando Lopez-Alves, special advisor of CEIEG as well as a professor of sociology at UC Santa Barbara. In Buenos Aires, the event was facilitated by Eric Arias, Rebeca Gonzalez Esteves, and Sebastian Kobaru.

In Delhi, the workshop was cosponsored by the Council for Social Development. We relied on the gracious hosting of Manoranjan Mohanty, who was a professor at the council as well as a fellow of the UC Santa Barbara Orfalea Center. Our thanks to the staff of the council, especially Prashant Trivedi who was instrumental with the workshop logistics, and to the staff of the India International Centre in New Delhi where the workshop was held.

In Cairo, we held two workshops, both facilitated by several UC Santa Barbara faculty members who were in residence in Egypt at the time: Juan Campo, Magda Campo, Nancy Gallagher, and Paul Amar. Juan Campo served as co-convenor of one of the workshops; Amar was co-convenor of the other and helped to arrange many of the speakers. The planning team for the Cairo workshop also involved Saad Ibrahim. We greatly appreciated the services of the staff of the American University at Cairo, and the facilities that AUC provided in their old campus adjacent to Tahrir Square.

The Shanghai workshop was cosponsored by the Center for Global Studies Center at Shanghai University, and its innovative director, Changgang Guo, served as co-convenor. At that time, Guo was also the dean of graduate studies at the University, and he contributed significantly to the planning for the workshop. We greatly appreciate the efforts of the Shanghai University staff, including Zhenghan Zhang, and the assistance of Collin Dvorak, a global studies graduate of UC-Santa Barbara and former assistant at the Orfalea Center who was a graduate student at Shanghai University at the time and cheerfully assisted in making arrangements and showing us around town.

In Moscow, our workshop was cosponsored by the School of Global Studies at Moscow University. The cohost and co-convenor of the workshop was Dean Ilya Ilyin. Central to the success of the workshop was Alexander Rosanov, who served as translator, guide, arranger, and friend. Other members of the Russian staff for the workshop included Ivan Aleshkovsky, who was involved in the early workshop planning, and Nicolai Zolotarev, who provided simultaneous translation.

We are most grateful for the time and effort of over a hundred scholars, policy-makers, and practitioners who participated in these eleven workshops. Their names and affiliation are cited in the participants list at the end of this book. Some traveled days to attend these sessions, and several were at multiple events. Each provided insights and wisdom that are reflected in the pages of this book, in the summary reports of each workshop that have been published by the Orfalea Center and which may be found in digital form on the center's website, and in the video clips that constitute the video archive of the project and are found on the website, www.orfaleacenter.ucsb.edu/luce.

Three of the participants served as special consultants outside the workshop format. Zhuo Xinping, the highest ranking scholar of religious studies in the Chinese Academy of Social Sciences, journeyed from Beijing to Santa Barbara so we could consult with him on issues relevant to the project. We are grateful that Craig Calhoun joined us in a panel discussion in Santa Barbara on a topic related to the project, even though at the time he was in the process of moving to London to become the new director of the London School of Economics. We were moved that Robert Bellah would find the topic of the project of sufficient interest to come from Berkeley to Santa Barbara to present a paper on the possibilities of global civil religion. The ideas in Bellah's paper are the substance of chapter 4 of this book. Sadly, this paper was one of his last, since he died suddenly in July 2013. We dedicate this book to Bellah's memory, not only because of the impact that the ideas in his paper had on our project, but also because of the way that his approach to the study of religion and society has informed our outlook on this subject as a whole. Bellah always took the wide view, historically and comparatively, in trying to understand the relationship between culture and society and between religion and social change. Thus, in a very real sense, this project is informed in every aspect by Bellah's scholarly sensibilities and his conviction that the study of religion in society will illumine the most significant depths of human imagination and aspiration.

As this manuscript came close to publication, we have had yet more people to thank. We would like to thank Maeve Cornell-Taylor, Jennifer Eastman, and Eric Schmidt at the University of California Press.

Finally, a word about how this book was crafted and what each of us did. We began with brainstorming sessions that included the three authors— Mark Juergensmeyer, Dinah Griego, and John Soboslai—along with center's program director, Victor Faessel; a key writer, John Ucciferri; and our videographer, Paul Lynch. We reviewed the videos and reports from the workshops and sifted through the many topics to come up with overarching themes. Eventually, it was Juergensmeyer's task to provide the narrative line for the book and to set out a general outline. Griego worked with the transcripts of the workshops, relating what was said to the ideas in the outline, and providing nuance and variation to the theme. Most of the writing was done by Juergensmeyer and Soboslai, with Soboslai working closely with Griego to make sure that the ideas were directly connected to the workshop discussions. Finally, each of us read everything—not once, but multiple times—arguing cheerfully over each chapter sometimes in person, sometimes digitally, sometimes by Skype, even when Griego was in Brazil, Juergensmeyer in Myanmar, and Soboslai in Connecticut. Juergensmeyer had the last reading and the last word, as it turned out, though each of us is to blame for it all. Though, in truth, it was less of a burden than a pleasure to work together on the completion of a project that had been so close to our lives for several years and that articulates some of the most critical issues of religion and social change in the tumult of our global age.

Tahrir Square, Cairo. Photograph by Dinah Griego.

Introduction

THINKING ABOUT RELIGION IN THE GLOBAL AGE

CAIRO'S TAHRIR SQUARE WAS FULL of life—flags waving, throngs of protestors and soccer fans, posters with political slogans, and loudspeakers screaming ardent speeches that called for freedom from oppression. It was one of many such rallies that followed the tumultuous sequence of public protests that had led to the ouster of the Mubarak regime on January 25, 2011.

But on this occasion, a group of scholars and activists were meeting at the same time and almost at the same place, in a university hall just off Tahrir Square. The meeting's participants could hear the shouts and speeches through the open windows as they discussed the momentous changes in Egyptian society, changes echoed throughout the Muslim world, and the significance that these changes had for our understanding of the role of religion in public life. It was as if reality was breaking through the walls to remind the discussants of the importance of the dramatic social and cultural changes in Egypt in the global era.

A similar meeting in New Delhi, India, was quieter, and yet outside the India International Center where the discussions took place were myriad changes. The city was being spruced up for the Commonwealth Games, a sort of smaller version of the Olympics, and the improvements were vivid: new roads and freeways, a high-speed subway system, and enormous new stadiums and sports pavilions. Alongside these public works were private ones, not just office buildings and apartments, but new Hindu temples as well, some of them associated with religious movements appealing especially to the mobile Indian middle class.

At Cairo and New Delhi, as at other meetings, including ones at Buenos Aires and Santa Barbara, much of the discussion in this series of workshops on the role of religion in global civil society was about the transformations of old religious institutions in the global age. In many cases, traditional religion had become politicized, in some cases fused with right-wing nationalism, as traditional leaders led the charge against pluralism and secularism and, in an era in which the nation-state is under siege, saw an opportunity for nationalism to be buttressed by religious ideologies and institutions.

At the Shanghai meeting, however, it was a different story. Religious groups countered the sterility of modern life. Outside the meeting's venue at Shanghai University, a dazzling modern city was being created. The vista one saw across the Huangpo River was the Pudong financial district, a vision of the future—shards of gleaming glass and metal skyscrapers reaching to the heavens in a profusion of imaginary architectural styles. But in the futuristic modernity of Shanghai, religion is making remarkable inroads. After decades of strict atheistic socialism, temples and mosques have been restored and are thriving. Christianity has become curiously popular, especially among educated youth. House churches and new religious movements challenge the government's attempts to control them. As workshop participant Xu Yihua, a professor at Shanghai's Fudan University, put it, religious belief in China "has been hidden but is now increasingly emergent."[1] In China, religious practices are becoming an alternative to the secular past.

Much the same can be said of Russia. In Moscow, the meetings were held on the campus of Lomonosov Moscow State University, which has, as its symbolic center of campus, an enormous Stalin-era structure—one of seven that were built at different locations in the city. It is an imposing, thirty-six-story edifice that merges a stern, socialist-era architectural style with almost wedding-cake elegance. It seemed paradoxical that discussions would be held on the changing role of religion—with Russian Orthodox priests and Muslim religious leaders in attendance—in the shadow of such a symbol of the atheistic ideological past, when Moscow was the centerpiece of the Soviet Union. But now, as in China, religion has become a resource for building a new society with an array of cultural diversity. On the one hand, religious ideas support a resurgent nationalism; on the other hand, they are windows to a wider world. This seems to be one of the contradictory themes of religion in the global era.

The meetings in Moscow, Shanghai, Cairo, New Delhi, Buenos Aires, and Santa Barbara were part of a project that spanned several years and aimed at assessing these and other aspects of the changing role of religion in public life around the world. With the support of the Henry Luce Foundation, we were able to bring together at each event an eclectic mix of journalists, social activists, religious leaders, and representatives of service organizations in the region—some twenty to thirty participants at each meeting. (The entire list of 160 may be found in the appendix to this book.) We tried to choose participants who came from differing professional backgrounds but who were sensitive to the social and religious changes in their region and articulate in expressing their observations.

We wanted to understand some of the great social changes that are occurring around the world in the opening years of the twenty-first century and the role that religion plays within them. We described this as a project exploring the role of religion in global civil society. By "civil society" we meant what the sociologist Peter Berger meant when he described it as a term that has come to signify all aspects of society that "stand in between the private sphere ... and the macro-institutions of the state and the economy."[2] The term is sometimes used in a more specific sense of the nongovernmental, nonprofit citizen movements and organizations that provide social services and promote a more humane society, and we were indeed interested in how religion related to these movements and organizations. But in a larger sense, we were interested in all aspects of society outside the arenas of government and business, not only in particular regions around the world, but also in global society as a whole. One of the questions that fascinated us was whether there is such a thing as "global civil religion," a nexus of moral and spiritual sensibilities in the global community that might be characterized as religious.

We described these meetings as "workshops," rather then "seminars" or "conferences." Seldom were formal papers presented. Instead, we asked the participants to write brief comments and enter into discussion around several central questions that we posed at each meeting. We first asked how society in each region is changing in the present era of globalization—a period roughly since the end of the Cold War in the last decade of the twentieth century. We then asked how religion—by which we meant religious institutions, ideas, leaders, cultures, and communities—was affected by these changes, and how it responded to them. And we wondered what the future might hold.

The authors of this book participated in these discussions, and in the pages that follow, we hope to give a sense of what was discovered as we attempted to take the temperature of religion at this moment in the global era. It is not a report, but a set of reflections based on the discussions in the workshops and the wider conversation about religion in the twenty-first century. It is clear that religion is not dead; how it lives and what it will become in the global era are the subjects we want to explore.

JUST WHAT DO YOU MEAN BY *RELIGION?*

Though the word *religion* was used frequently in the discussions in this project, rarely did anyone interrupt the flow of conversation to say, "now just what do you mean by that?" This was fortunate, since arguments about the definition of *religion* can be tedious and often ultimately pointless. In most cases, it is self-evident what *religion* means in the context in which the word is used. Religious organizations, leaders, and ideologies, for instance, wear their labels on their sleeves, and you know them when you see them.

When it comes to religious cultures and attitudes, however, what is religious or not is a more complicated matter. In the 2013 protests in Istanbul's Taksim Square, one of the motivating forces behind many of the protestors was the fear that the ruling party in Turkey was trying to religionize politics and transform the secular society of Ataturk's vision for the country into something more Islamic. What the young people in Taksim Square had in mind was the array of personal liberties and moral choices that were previously allowed in the more permissive society of urban Turkey. These personal freedoms were not necessarily antireligious, of course, but they were often perceived that way, by both the secular protestors and the religious defendants of a more traditional order. In this case, religion was seen by the protestors as part of an intrusive way of reconceiving individuals' relationship to society and their obligations to it by equating public morality with religious virtue.

In Egypt, where society has been predominantly religious, not secular, for years, the issue was one of degrees of religiosity. It is safe to say that social mores in Egypt, even in cities, are stricter than those of urban Turkey. The rise of a new religiously based party—such as the short-lived reign of the Muslim Brotherhood's Freedom and Justice Party following the 2012 elections—raises questions about how religious the country's politics should be and to what degree religiosity should be associated with attitudes that limit personal freedoms and restrict the range of religious expression. Interestingly, in Egypt, the clergy, by and large, have stayed out of politics. When we met with the chief cleric in Egypt, the Grand Mufti, in his comfortable offices adjoining a mosque in Cairo, he expressed fears that the Muslim Brotherhood—an organization led by middle-class Muslim businessmen and professionals—would drag religion into the dirty mire of political squabbles, and he wanted no part of it. So in Egypt it is more difficult to say just what is and is not the religious perspective on political life.

In many parts of the world, there is a great deal of ambiguity about what is religious or not religious with regard to a particular position or worldview. One of the participants in the discussions, Jacob Olupona, a historian of religion who teaches at Harvard, commented about his native Nigeria when he said, in describing the often savage encounters between Christians and Muslim groups in northern Nigeria, "as bad as the situation is in Nigeria, we are not too sure whether what we are seeing is political, is economic, or even is religious."[3]

In Bangladesh, however, the lines between religion and politics are blurry, because everything is viewed as religious, according to Lamia Karim, an American participant who was raised in Bangladesh and who is part of the large social service network, the Center for the Study of Women in Society. She expressed frustration about the way that many of her kinfolk in Bangladesh fail to grasp the concept of secularism—by which she meant keeping religious values from interfering with public policy. "Frankly speaking," she said, "there is a silent revolution happening in Bangladesh, and it's not secular."[4] Her concern is not only about the presuppositions that terms like *religious* or *secular* carry but also that they not be used to prejudge the situations to which they refer.

Yet Lamia Karim's observation raises an interesting question: are the terms *secular* and *religious* applicable to traditional cultures in which religious images, values, and virtues are infused in so many aspects of public life? According to Delhi workshop participant Manindra Thakur, associate professor at the Center for Political Studies at Jawaharlal Nehru University, part of the problem is linguistic. "The English language," Thakur said, "has this problem of talking of everything in either/or terms, and therefore it fails to capture that we are secular and religious simultaneously."[5] It is the language that we employ that does not allow for shades of difference between secular and sacred, that fails to appreciate what Thakur describes as the coexistence of the secular and religious in many locales.

In recent years there has been considerable discussion in American and European scholarly circles about the concepts of religion and secularism, and many scholars agree with the point that the Indian scholar made, that there is a linguistic problem with the terms. A task force of the Social Science Research Council in New York convened a multiyear project on rethinking secularism and concluded that secularism is itself something—it is not just the absence of religion. It is a worldview laden with value assumptions about the nature of the self and its relationship to society.[6] This means that the idea of secular society itself can be a challenge to traditional religious worldviews. The two are seen as competitive.

In fact, the competition between secularism and religion was integral to the creation of these concepts. In seventeenth- and eighteenth-century Europe, when the terms came into common use, secularism was thought to be an ideology of order that would replace religion as the central force in organizing society. Instead of religion informing public values and ideals, rational thought would be the only true measure of the value of social goals. In France, abandoned churches were turned into "temples of reason" to celebrate this transformation. Interestingly, this competition between reason and religion is also symbolized today when churches are converted into secular commercial or public purposes. In the English city of Oxford, for instance, an old Methodist church building has been turned into a lively pub called "Freud's."

But it was not just the buildings that illustrated the way that secularism was replacing religion during the Enlightenment. The underlying notions of social morality that are contained in traditional religious laws and outlooks were replaced by Enlightenment notions of a moral community that would undergird secular social and political life. For this reason—in France, England, the United States, and elsewhere in the Western world—the role of religion was restricted to the rites and beliefs of churches, which were consequently relegated to the margins of public life. They were to be enjoyed on Sunday and forgotten for the rest of the week.

This marginalization of religion never worked perfectly in the West. Religious societies embracing religious values in public life cropped up religious communities of all sizes, from the small New Harmony colony in nineteenth-century Indiana to the large Mormon community that developed in Utah and spread throughout the western United States. Elsewhere in the world, the secularization that came with European colonialism was never completely integrated. In India, as Rounaq Jahan, one of the Delhi seminar participants, explained, secularism does not mean what it means in Europe and America. It does not imply a separation of government and religion, but rather the *equal treatment* of all religious communities by the government. Jahan, who is distinguished fellow at the Centre for Policy Dialogue at Dhaka, Bangladesh, and senior research scholar at Columbia University's School of International and Public Affairs, said that in South Asia, the common thinking is not "completely divorcing state from church." Rather, she explained, the idea of secularism in India, Pakistan, Bangladesh, and Nepal is that the state—and all citizens, for that matter—should "tolerate everybody, give equal voice" and not stifle anyone's freedom of expression.[7] Hence the Indian government is free to help to build and protect temples and mosques, for instance, and to oversee the elections of administrators of Sikh shrines, so long as it treats all religious communities equally, preferring none over the others. That is what secularism in India means.

In other parts of the world, communities of people are increasingly turning toward traditional religion to find ways of thinking about the moral basis for social and political order when secular politics seems to have lost its moral bearings. Ravi Bhatia, retired Delhi University professor and executive member of the International Peace Research Association, who was one of the participants at the Delhi seminar, observed that "the social fabric is breaking apart" in a time of urbanization and globalization. And increasingly, in the wake of that social breakdown, in South Asia as elsewhere, it is "religion that is going to be an alternative."[8] This appears to be a global phenomenon: religion enters politics when the old secular politics seems corrupt or insufficient. There is what one of the authors of this book has described elsewhere as "a loss of faith in secular nationalism."[9]

LIVING THE DICHOTOMY AND LOVING IT

The assertion that religion is *not* separate from politics is a real kick in the pants to the Enlightenment notion of the dichotomy between religion and secular life. For a couple of centuries, at least in the cultures directly affected by Europe and America, we had learned to live with the dichotomy. Some of us even embraced it.

The idea of the dichotomy is pretty simple. Before the rise of the European Enlightenment ways of thinking in the eighteenth century, religion (or what was thought to be religious culture and religious civilization) was seamlessly a part of the larger culture of a society. There was only one culture, one morality, and one set of public virtues; religious ideas and traditions were part of all of them. The nineteenth-century economist Adam Smith was a theologian as well as a moral philosopher. The nineteenth-century biologist Charles Darwin also had been trained in theology. As the historian of religion Wilfred Cantwell Smith pointed out, the very term *religion* was seldom used, since there was nothing to contrast it with.[10] People used terms such as *tradition, faith,* and *belief,* and they recognized the autonomy of the religious institutions of church and temple, but there was no concept of a separate religious worldview that needed a name. There was no need for the word *religion.*

Enlightenment thinking provided a different way of viewing the situation: the public life of societies was essentially secular—untouched by the beliefs, traditions, rituals, and clerical power associated with religious institutions—and religion was something that you did on your day off. A whole new concept was created—religion—along with the concept of the secular, and these were thought to demarcate two spheres of being. When you were in public life, voting and arguing and creating rules for society, you were secular. When you were at home or in church, you could turn to religion—or choose not to. It was something private and personal. As the rationalist and psychologist of religion William James once put it, religion is something that humans do "in their solitude."[11]

If religion was seen as a private experience, that meant that the task of providing for social morality and communal cohesion was transferred to secular society. It has been a heavy weight to bear. A group of French intellectuals in the nineteenth century invented the idea of "ideologies," systems of secular ideas and values that would replace the social morality of religion. The sense of social cohesion was provided by nationalism, an idea that swept the world in the nineteenth and twentieth centuries. The French social analyst Alexis de Tocqueville regarded nationalism as a kind of "new religion." The extreme forms of nationalism did indeed take on an aura of sacredness; they commanded exclusive allegiance and challenged any other forms of voluntary association, including religious ones. During the mid-twentieth century, nationalist ideologies—linked with Italian fascism, German national socialism, and Stalin's narrow view of state socialism in the Communist Soviet Union—were enemies of both religion and the moderate nationalism of most nation-states.

In most parts of the world where the secular nation-state idea took hold, a fairly comfortable relationship developed between secular politics and organized religion. Secular leaders did not have to worry about whether they were in conformity with religious teachings and values, and religious leaders did not have to take responsibility for maintaining social order and giving moral direction to public life. Both sides seemed to have learned to live with the dichotomy and to benefit from it.

Even in the non-Western parts of the world, which were not direct inheritors of the Enlightenment's dichotomous secular-religious way of thinking, a form of secularism took root. As we have noted in the India case, secularism provided a neutral governance structure over a society deeply divided along the lines of religious communities. In India, Muslims, Hindus, Sikhs, and Christians could all go about their merry lives, equally supported by government institutions, assured that their central government favored no one religious group over any other. This neutrality is what secularism in India means. In countries like Turkey, Egypt, and prerevolution Iran, however, political leaders embraced a philosophy of secularism not only to keep a distance between quarrelling religious camps, each with its own perspective on what was proper for society, but also because they thought that the secular worldview was the modern one, the wave of the future, and they were eager to put their societies on the path of the secular future rather than the religious past. Secularity did not mean, as in the Indian case, equal support of all religions. It meant the subordinate status of all religions to the program of modernization.

So what began to go wrong? What happened at the end of the twentieth century and the rise of the twenty-first that allowed for the rise of a strident new religiosity that put religious activists into direct confrontation with secular politics?

It could all be coincidence. Perhaps all of these movements of religious activism around the world, in every region, associated with every religious tradition, emerged at the same time at the end of the twentieth century by chance. New religious movements in Japan, militant Hindus and Sikhs, radical Muslims and angry Christians—there have always been some of these in all times and places, and maybe what appears to be a sudden rise of so many—and in such an aggressive manner—might only be a fluke of history.

Perhaps. Or there could be something going on, something of a virtually global nature that affects all cultures and areas of the planet.

The word *global* is a clue to what this might be. The end of the Cold War in the last decade of the twentieth century signaled the ending of one worldwide era and the beginning of another. What ended was the contestation between forms of nationalism and supernationalism that characterized the major world wars of the twentieth century—World War I, World War II, and the Cold War. Some observers thought that this meant that the West had won, ideological conflicts were a thing of the past, and we were witnessing "the end of history," as Francis Fukuyama called it.[12] In truth, the situation was more complicated.

Two things were happening around the world, and they were related. The first was the loss of faith in secular nationalism, which began developing after the end of colonialism in the mid-twentieth century and the creation of many new nation-states. These secular entities were not always able to live up to their own materialistic expectations of wealth and progress. More disturbing, they did not seem capable of stopping the greed and corruption of individuals' attempts to gain from the system. They seemed to be entities without a moral compass, something religion had provided in the past.

At the same time, globalization emerged as a new framework of interaction that bypassed the nation-state. Transnational economic production, distribution, and financing were all conducted outside the limits of national control. Simultaneously, global forms of communication and transportation put everyone in contact with everyone. Social awareness exploded from its local confines into a global arena. The march of globalization added further to the weakening of national identities and local forms of control.

It was in the rubble of fading secular nationalism that new claims of national identity based on religion and ethnicity appeared. On the one hand, they helped to rescue the idea of nationalism by reasserting a religious basis for national communities when secularism failed to provide that communal vision. On the other hand, they produced new tensions, since not everyone within a society would agree on what form of religion should be normative and which religious leaders and groups should be accorded privilege within the new religious nationalism.

The problem was that religion had reentered public life, but it was not the same religiosity of the pre-Enlightenment worldview. The old notions of religious society allowed for a great deal of diversity within them, and different sects of Islam or Hinduism, for instance, could happily coexist before the partition of South Asia into India and Pakistan. India's earlier religious history is a tapestry of different faiths, as was the case in much of Asia. When the Mongol armies spread out from Central Asia in the thirteenth and fourteenth centuries CE to create the largest land empire in history, leaders such as Genghis Khan and Kublai Khan were remarkably tolerant in their views of local cultures and diverse religious affiliations. A different empire, the

Moghul rule in sixteenth- and seventeenth-century India, famously tolerated a diversity of faiths, and the great emperor Akbar was said to welcome theologians from Christian, Sikh, Hindu, Buddhist, and Muslim traditions to expound their ideas in his court as he challenged them in scholarly debate.

But the nineteenth- and twentieth-century post-Enlightenment view of religion was more narrow. Since religious organizations were marginalized from a central role in society, contending versions of Islam, Christianity, or Buddhism clashed among themselves. These were the forms of religion that rose up at the end of the twentieth century to reclaim society in the name of religion, but it was in the name of their narrow views of what the faiths entailed.

So here we are at the beginning of the twenty-first century. Religion is once again playing a role in public life. But it is a fractured and confused role, in part because of the narrow way that religious groups and organizations have evolved in recent centuries, and in part because of the chaotic nature of this moment in global social transformation. To understand how religious groups have responded to it, have been shaped by it, and have tried to change it, we have to look first more closely at the turmoil at the transition to the global age of the twenty-first century. It is to these developments that we will now turn.

Temple construction, Shanghai. Photograph by Paul Lynch.

ONE

The Social Turmoil of the Twenty-First Century

CRISES OF IDENTITY, ACCOUNTABILITY, AND SECURITY

VISITING THE OLD CAMPUS OF Shanghai University in the heart of the city is like taking a trip back in time. The red-brick buildings are neatly arranged around a central campus lawn, with wide walkways lined by old trees. The buildings' turreted walls remind one of what the student ambience must have been like in the 1920s, when the university was founded as a rival to the missionary colleges that were sprouting up throughout China. The Baptist missionary organization had created a college with a similar name, the University of Shanghai (now merged with East China Normal University), which was meant to be a Christian witness to the Chinese people. It was part of the great missionary movement that swept out from America and Europe and encircled the world, with the dream of making a distinctly Western form of Protestant religiosity the global norm.

That did not happen, of course, though there were a few converts, and a fledgling Christian community blossomed. But the movement spurred educated Chinese into creating their own independent universities, and the old Yanchang campus of Shanghai University is a monument to an earlier generation's dream of modern education. Later it was socialist education that dominated the curriculum, as China became part of the global socialist milieu. Today, however, the campus is surrounded by symbols of yet another globalization, a new economic one. The sleepy red-brick campus is dwarfed by a circle of high-rise buildings and brightly lit shops. The stores announce their wares for an upscale, globalized clientele: scarves from Hermès, handbags from Louis Vuitton, and watches from Rolex.

These days very few students actually study at the old campus of Shanghai University. The small campus has been abandoned for a new location ten kilometers north, the bustling Baoshan campus, itself something of a small city of high-rise buildings of modern architectural design. Over forty thousand students are enrolled, a fourth of them in graduate and professional schools. Shanghai University has become a part of contemporary China, and that means being open to new ideas and commercial possibilities from around the world. It is also increasingly attracting international students, including many from the United States and Europe.

In response, the university has created new graduate programs in English, international business, and international finance. It has also created a global studies graduate program and a center for the study of global affairs. Shanghai University was the first in the country to embrace global studies as a field; others have more recently been established in Beijing and Shantou.

What has come to Shanghai University is not only global studies but also globalization as a phenomenon, as it has to the rest of Shanghai. The municipality has, after a few decades of astounding growth, become one of the world's great global cities. If you stand at the bund—the levee at the edge of the Huangpu River that lines the downtown area of old Shanghai—and look behind you, you will see a wall of old British buildings that were once the most important in the city. Twenty years ago, that was the heart of Shanghai, and when you looked across the river, you saw a few buildings, but mostly rice paddies and empty fields. Today the Pudong region across the river has one of the world's most impressive skylines. At the center of the forest of skyscrapers is the 121-story Shanghai Tower, reaching, it seems, halfway to the moon; it is the tallest in China and, for a time, the second tallest building in the world, after the Burj Khalifa in Dubai.

The building boom in Shanghai is entirely due to the globalization of production and trade that has made China one of the world's largest producers of consumer goods. The boom began when globalization began, in the last decade of the twentieth century. This was also, according to the *New York Times* columnist Tom Friedman, the true beginning of the twenty-first century.[1] The fall of the Berlin Wall in 1989 marked the end of the Cold War and the beginning of the global era. Even before that date, however, the world had begun to change in profound ways. The softening of the divide between the Communist and non-Communist worlds was only part of the transformation. A more significant dimension was the rise of new transnational forms of economic production, distribution, and financing, coupled with the instant communications of the internet and massive demographic shifts made possible through the easing of travel restrictions and the rise of inexpensive air travel.

On the one hand, the era of globalization provided new opportunities. Take cell phones, for instance. Twenty years ago in rural China, telephones were virtually nonexistent. Today even the remote pedicab driver has one in his hand. The world is at his fingertips. Computer technology has made low-cost, worldwide communication available to nearly everyone. Relatively inexpensive goods produced through global production networks are sold everywhere to a grateful consumer public—who try to ignore the harsh realities of workplaces such as the Foxconn factory in Shenzhen, China, and the troublesome labor conditions around the world. Accompanying this global consumerism, a whole new generation of global youth emerged who shared a common popular culture of music, videos, and fashion. Rural teenagers in China's Xinjiang Province insist on wearing Nike shoes. Globalization has, in a sense, pulled the world more closely together.

On the other hand, there are new problems. The ease of mobility and transportation, coupled with the erosion of the power of the nation-state, undercuts national identities. The same Nike-wearing teenager in Xinjiang might very well be participating in protests against what he and his friends regard as the Chinese central government's incursion into traditional Uighur Muslim culture. At the same time, the emergence of transnational economic and organizational networks that are outside the control of national governments create new challenges of accountability. The fear of many Chinese government officials about the Muslim protests in western China is that they might be connected with the strident jihadi ideology of Muslim extremism that has troubled other parts of the world in the late twentieth and early twenty-first centuries. The spread of radical ideologies associated with terrorism and the potential for environmental and other disasters on a global scale have produced new concerns about public security.

In the global era, then, these have been the critical issues: identity, accountability, and security. Each of these touches on religion in some way, and for each of them, religious ideas and communities have provided solutions. In the remainder of this chapter we will look at the religious aspects of each of these global issues in turn.

SEARCHING FOR SOCIAL IDENTITIES

One of the participants in both our Delhi and Santa Barbara seminars is a prominent Indian scholar who studied at Berkeley before establishing his career at Delhi University. He speaks fluent Chinese and for years has done research in a region in China that is part of a larger project on Chinese-Indian comparative development. So he travels frequently to China. But he also travels frequently to the United States, since both of his children came to America for higher education and have settled into comfortable careers in California and New Jersey. Their families are well established here, and their children are being raised as American kids.

So we asked him, "With what country do you identify—India, China, or the United States?" "I am Indian, of course," he said, "and proudly so. But my heart is also in China and the United States." And then he added, "I guess I am becoming a citizen of the world."

His story has become a common one. The increasing mobility of people and the ease of global communications make it possible for everyone to live everywhere, while maintaining contacts with family and friends who may be living everywhere else. As a result, huge new multicultural populations are emerging around the world that have mixed identities—grounded in their new homelands but in touch with traditional regions that are often beyond the seas.

Take Southern California as an example. The greater Los Angeles area is home to over 600,000 residents of Filipino ancestry. This makes it the largest Filipino city outside of the Philippines, and the seventh largest Filipino city in the world. In addition, over 500,000 Persians live in the greater Los Angeles area, a number equal to the twelfth largest city in Iran. And over 3.5 million people in the greater Los Angeles area are of Mexican ancestry, which makes Los Angeles the second largest Mexican city in the world. Also living in Southern California are massive numbers of Chinese, Vietnamese, Indonesian, Thai, Asian Indians, Pakistanis, Bangladeshis, Sri Lankans, Africans, newly migrated Europeans, and members of various Middle East, Caribbean, and South American communities. Los Angeles is truly a global city, and it is a microcosm of the world's diverse nationalities.

People who pull up stakes and move to Los Angeles and other parts of the world are often divided in their loyalties between their new homes and their familiar ground. But even people who do not move are affected by globalization's assault on traditional national identities. The effect of globalization on Thai nationalism was observed by one of our seminar participants, Surichai Wun'gaeo, director of the Center for Peace and Conflict Studies and professor of sociology at Chulalongkorn University in Bangkok, Thailand, who remarked that even rural Thai people are challenged by globalization and that people around the world are no longer "trapped by national identities," because increasingly they participate in global economic production and distribution chains.[2]

But it is not just economic change that is undermining traditional national allegiances. The mass media of videos, television, and movies, along with social networks provided by the internet, also challenge the usual lines of national communication. The political scientist Karl Deutsch once observed that national cohesion is built upon the national integration of communications networks.[3] In an age of global communication, therefore, these nationalist ties are broken and, in some cases, all but obliterated. As distinguished Indian political scientist J. P. S. Uberoi noted in our Delhi seminar, today one's social identity is fluid, determined in part by changing global circumstances.[4]

National identities persist, of course. This is especially so during international sporting events, such as the Olympics or the World Cup, when nationalistic loyalties merge with the fanaticism of sports enthusiasm. But nationalism can also emerge at other times, in surprising moments. Russia, after the collapse of the Soviet Union, went through a new burst of nationalism, one in which the Russian Orthodox Church played a significant role. Indonesia, after the departure of the Dutch colonial rule, seemed destined for disintegration, since it was a somewhat artificially created unity of over seventeen thousand islands. At present, the sense of national unity in Indonesia seems to be enjoying a new popularity, fueled in part by religious leaders seeking to promote their positions through nationalist politics.

Yet it is also true that the global era is a time when the notion of the nation-state is under stress. This is an occasion for other social identities to come to the fore, often with political force. After the U.S.-led military invasion toppled the secular regime of Saddam Hussein in Iraq in 2003, the strident new politics of the country crystallized around religious and ethnic identities—Sunni Arabs, Shi'a Arabs, and Kurds—and the insurgency led by the movement called the Islamic State in Iraq and Syria in 2014 was determined to tear the nation apart. When one of the authors of this book interviewed Iraqi leaders in Baghdad in 2004, the affiliates of religious parties said that they believed in a united Iraq, but they wanted to make sure that their communities were in what they regarded as their proper leadership roles within the new society. The leaders of each of the communities magnified their own group's importance in Iraq's new political configuration, leading to internal squabbles and worse—violent ethnic strife that came to a head in the 2014 conflict. In the aftermath of the secular nationalism of Saddam Hussein's Ba'ath Party, each group wanted a religious and ethnic nationalism that would reflect its own sense of communal identity.

The quest for social identity in an era of globalization has led to a paradox with regard to nationalism and the idea of national community. On the one hand, the idea of a single national identity is weakened in an era of globalization in which competing social identities are easily available through, for instance, communications media. China has been notorious in its attempts to control its citizens' access to media from outside. On the other hand, the challenges of globalization can foster a sense of national pride over what is distinctive about a national culture in the homogeneity of global society. This nationalism can flourish when it is fused with the dominant religious identity of the nation.

An example of this revival of nationalism in religious form is found in several countries in South Asia. Pakistan, for instance, was intended to be a secular state. Muhammad Ali Jinnah, a founder of the nation, was a refined lawyer who had lived in London and became leader of the Muslim League, the political voice of the Muslim community in South Asia during the last years of British colonial rule. He was a quintessential cosmopolitan, who had no desire to create a state based solely on religious ideas. But Jinnah was also determined to protect the Muslim community against what he perceived to be a hidden pro-Hindu agenda in the politics of the nominally secular Congress Party in India. What he initially wanted was a kind of federal system in India that would allow Muslim-dominated regions to have more autonomy in a unified India. What he got when the British withdrew was a whole new nation based on a shared religious identity and political leaders who used religion as a way of shoring up their own nationalist credentials.

Perhaps no political leader in Pakistan did more to pander to conservative Muslim support than Muhammad Zia-ul-Haq, who led the country from 1977 to 1988, after instituting a coup against his mentor, Zulfikar Ali Bhutto. Zia established shari'ah law, outlawed marginal and heretical religious movements, and subsidized the mujahideen against the Soviet-backed government in neighboring Afghanistan. One legacy of the Zia regime has been the covert Pakistani support for extremist Muslim political movements in Afghanistan. First the mujahideen and then the Taliban have been quietly supported by elements of the Pakistan military and intelligence services. The ideas of the Taliban are related to the Deoband Muslim reform movement in South Asia, which attempted to purify and standardize the teachings and practices of Islam. These reforms were interpreted by groups such as the Taliban in a rigid and uncompromising way. The movement was not only an agent of religious standardization but also became the political wing of the Pashtun tribal community, large numbers of which were within Pakistan's own western borders. Mollifying the Taliban, then, was a way of currying favor with the critical Pashtun community.

At the same time that Pakistan was developing a more strident Muslim political posture, religious nationalism was also surfacing within India. In some ways, the emergence of the Bharatiya Janata Party (BJP) in the 1990s was the reemergence of a religious strand of Indian nationalism that extended back to the early part of the twentieth century. One of the early voices for Indian independence came from Vinayak Damodar Savarkar, president of the Hindu Mahasabha and advocated a concept of Hindu culture that he called *Hindutva* as being the basis of Indian national identity. He once entered into a debate with Mohandas Gandhi over the efficacy of using violence in the struggle for India's freedom.[5] Despite Savarkar's efforts, Hindu nationalism was not a major element in India's nationalist movement. After independence, several political parties took up the banner of support for Hindu causes, notably the Jan Sangh, but it was not until the 1990s that a new movement of religious consciousness led to spectacular political successes for the BJP.

The BJP was officially launched in 1980 out of the remnants of previous Hindu-oriented political parties.[6] It did not gain strength, however, until after the 1992 attack on a Muslim mosque in the town of Ayodhya. Religious activists associated with two sectarian Hindu organizations, the Vishwa Hindu Parishad and the Rashtriya Swayamsevak Sangh, championed the destruction of the mosque in order to liberate the grounds on which an ancient Hindu temple was said to have been located, a temple that marked the holy site of the god Ram's birth. Though archeologists questioned the authenticity of the assertion, and many questioned whether a spiritual entity such as a god actually had a birthplace, the site became a matter of religious contention, fueled by political rhetoric. It was the secular Congress Party that allowed the mosque to continue to exist on that spot. Though the Indian government said that it was protecting the site in the name of secularism— which in India meant the equal protection of all religious communities—the BJP political response was that the Congress Party's position was "pseudo-secularism" that, in fact, masked the privileging of minority communities such as Muslims over the interests of Hindus. (Even after the creation of

Pakistan, Muslims formed 15 percent of the population of India, enough to constitute a significant electoral base of votes, and a reason for politicians to curry Muslims' favor.)

On December 6, 1992, a mob of over a hundred thousand angry Hindus convened in Ayodhya, attacked the mosque with improvised tools, and rendered it to dust. The BJP capitalized on this sentiment of Hindu nationalism and, employing Savarkar's concept of Hindutva as the bedrock of Hindu nationalist culture, launched a series of political campaigns. The elections brought the BJP into positions of power in the legislatures of several states, and from 1998 to 2004 they were the dominant party in a national coalition that ruled India, and the BJP leader, Atal Bihari Vajpayee, became India's prime minister. In the May 2014 elections, the BJP again vaulted into power, this time without the need of a coalition to form the government, and the charismatic and controversial Narendra Modi—who had been accused of inflaming the anti-Muslim riots when he was chief minister of Gujarat in 2002—became prime minister. Modi was a member of the Hindu nationalist movement the Rashtriya Swayamsevak Sangh, and if one considers his party, the BJP, to be the political arm of Hindu nationalism in India, it quite likely has had the largest following of any religious nationalist movement in world history and has been one of the most politically successful. In the 2014 elections, over 170 million Indians voted for the BJP and, although it received only 31 percent of the total vote in a fragmented political race, it was able to capture the majority of seats in parliament.

According to one of the participants in our Delhi seminar, I. A. Rehman, who was a founding member of the Pakistan-India Human Rights Commission, the religionization of politics in India and Pakistan has had international repercussions and has poisoned the relations between the two countries. According to Rehman, "Pakistanis do not look on the Indians as Indian citizens of a neighboring country, they look upon the Indians as Hindus, [with] whom they have had long fights." Then he added, with a touch of sadness in his voice, "The whole concept of togetherness, and the syncretic tradition, which used to be the hallmark of the subcontinent in the sixteenth, seventeenth, and the beginning of the eighteenth centuries, was destroyed by the communalization of politics."[7]

Hence religion can become a problematic aspect of national identity. It can challenge secular nationalism by providing an alternate locus of identity, sometimes reviving nationalism in a troublesome religio-nationalist framework. The BJP form of religious nationalism is a mild version of even more strident religio-political movements found elsewhere in the world, such as the reign of the mullahs in post-revolutionary Iran. When political ideologies are linked with religious beliefs, boundaries are sharpened and realigned around what people believe, rather than joint participation in improving life for a common community. When religion combines with nationality, it strengthens ties between some while marginalizing others through legislation and public opinion.

Religious nationalism can marginalize groups that do not share the faith of the dominant community. In Pakistan this is particularly a problem for the small Christian minority, many of whom come from families who were lower-caste converts early in the twentieth century. Now they are seen as remnants of that colonial period, and worse—sometimes portrayed as agents of American and European imperialism. Those exclusionary measures are also connected to larger programs of international concern. Rehman noted that Pakistan's "strong anti-West feeling" leads many people in the country to see Christian minorities as "Western agents."[8] Simply by being Christian they are assumed to be cooperating with an enemy and thus are regarded as enemies themselves.

In Egypt, the Coptic Christian minority has suffered outbreaks of violence since the 1970s. Then president Anwar el-Sadat made overtures to Islamic leaders to bolster support for his administration, and nationalist fervor became wrapped in an Islamic piety that excluded Christians from the national conversation. Their identity as Copts overshadowed their identity as Egyptians. Under Hosni Mubarak, the Egyptian state embarked on a program of directly marginalizing Copts in response to a perceived danger from Christian authorities, and the Coptic communities unsurprisingly played a role in the removal of Mubarak and then of Mohammed Morsi from power in 2013. Since then, attacks on Coptic Christian homes and churches have continued, serving to further alienate the community from the state. A country that defines itself in religious terms sometimes prevents the full participation of citizens that profess a minority faith, leaving them unsure of the extent to which they can or should claim a national identity.

In the Egyptian case, however, Amr Abdulrahman, a doctoral researcher at Essex University, sees reason for hope. Since the 2011 Arab Spring uprising, there have been new opportunities for Coptic youth to participate in politics. Their independent political aspirations, however, have created tensions between young lay Christians and the Coptic Church authorities in Egypt. The elders think that the Coptic community is stronger if it unites behind its own leadership and speaks with one voice, but young Copts often articulate their own concerns. According to Abdulrahman, "even the political movements that tend to define themselves as Copts ... are not following the church."[9] Though the situation in Egypt is volatile and frequently changing, the renewed focus on national identity that resulted from the Arab Spring may offer a new space for citizens of all religions to have a voice in the public square. In the global era, identity—in its personal, social, political, ethnic, and religious dimensions—is a critical issue.

WONDERING WHO IS IN CHARGE

The second global issue is the problem of authority—knowing who is in charge. In the nation-state model of the twentieth century, U.S. president Harry S. Truman famously claimed his national authority: "the buck stops here." But in a global era, it's less clear where the buck stops. After World War II, it appeared as if the globe had become neatly carved into nation-state territories, each with its distinct area of control. Governments of each nation supposedly controlled that nation's economy and regulated commerce and communications within its sphere. We use the word, *supposedly*, since there were already networks of economic dependency, and that influence meant that many undeveloped nations were not as independent as they might have liked to be. Still, the general impression was that each state ran its own affairs.

In the global era, it is hard to say where the affairs of one nation end and the sphere of another begins. Manufacturing is a good example. Take the iconic figure of a Barbie doll: the plastic doll was designed in the United States and originally made in Hong Kong—later manufactured in China and elsewhere. Parts of the fabric for the costumes, the hair, and other items come from Malaysia, the Philippines, and myriad places around the world. The doll is sold in 150 countries and designed to fit fifty different ethnicities and nationalities. It is no longer clear whom Barbie represents or which country is solely responsible for its manufacture. Who is in charge of the Barbie doll?

The economics of particular countries have become interwoven with others through trade and the supply chains of global manufacturing, and that interdependency extends into other spheres, like food exports, communications, environmental concerns, and national securities. No nation is an economic island. The collapse of the Malaysian economy in 1997–1998 had a ripple effect throughout Southeast Asia, and around the world, economies from Russia to Iceland were affected. The affairs of one country have consequences that reach far beyond their borders, and naturally, people in those affected foreign countries want a voice in the decisions. The rise of international and transnational coordinating entities such as the World Trade Organization are attempts to provide at least the semblance of order in the new global economy. The post-World War II nation-state system has struggled to adjust to this new state of affairs, which, in turn, has left many citizens unsure as to who is in charge. To many, the global economy looks as out of control as the old Wild West.

For most of history, you could discover who was in charge simply by seeing who was using force to maintain control. During the great colonial era, European powers held sway in many parts of Asia, Africa, Latin America, and the Middle East. Their military might predominated. Since the middle of the twentieth century—the international period of world history—each nation was presumed to control its own affairs and had its own military force. France was in charge of France; Japan was in charge of Japan. Standing armies maintained control, and in some cases—especially in former colonial countries that had a weak internal political infrastructure, such as Egypt and Iraq—the rule was imposed harshly by military dictators.

In the global era of the twenty-first century, this international system of separate nation-states is under stress, not only because of the forces of globalization that have made economics, cultures, and communication systems intertwined, but also because of rising disaffection within those countries over the secular nationalist regimes that control them. Military regimes have been divided within themselves, and force has more often been used against rival political groups than it has against alien forces from the outside. The 1978 Islamic revolution in Iran is an example of such internal revolts—one where secular nationalism was the target. The success of the Ayatollah Khomeini's Islamic Revolution hit the secular world by surprise, and the reign of the Iranian mullahs was widely predicted to fail in a matter of months. But it endured—and turned out to be the harbinger of many other religio-political movements to come.

By the second decade of the twenty-first century, many people around the world, especially in Africa and the Middle East, had risen against the totalitarian governments that wielded unchecked violence against their populaces. The Arab Spring turned out to be a Global Spring. Anti-authoritarian movements around the world were motivated by a variety of factors to seek a voice in public affairs, and several of these movements involved contests over political control that resulted in bloody civil wars. Increasingly, the standing armies of nation-states have been used not to defend a country against outside aggressors but to quell insurrections within their own borders and shore up shaky regimes.

In places like Syria, the bloodshed continued for years, while in other places, like Libya, the result was the toppling of a dictatorship and the election of a General National Congress to govern the newly liberated nation. Troubles continued in Libya, however, in the form of armed groups prohibiting any officials who served under the old administration from holding a position in the new. A similar narrow-mindedness steered the Shi'a government of Prime Minister Nouri al-Maliki in Iraq in disastrous directions and led to his downfall in 2014. The question of leadership—and who can legitimately hold an office—is being negotiated in law courts and in the courts of public opinion in many of these postrevolutionary countries. In these negotiations, religious associations can give support to or detract from the legitimacy of governments, and leaders can be embraced by the new administrations or set up their own poles of authority.

The push for democracy itself can be reinforced or thwarted by religious institutions. In some cases, opposing sides find themselves benefiting from the advances of their opponent. Such a dynamic is evident in Indonesia, according to Mark Woodward, a participant in the South and Southeast Asia seminar, who is a leading authority on Indonesian religion and politics and who holds teaching posts at Arizona State University as well as at Gadjah Mada University and Sunan Kalijaga State Islamic University, both in Yogyakarta, Indonesia. Woodward explained that both liberal and conservative visions of Islam have gained a voice through the challenge to Indonesia's traditional political and social leadership. Woodward observed that the rise of new Islamic politics in Indonesia was directly related to the political challenges, and "it was the political transition that really opened everything in Indonesia." As a result, according to Woodward, "very conservative types of Islam came to occupy a place in public life where that had not been possible for the previous thirty years."[10] The democratic surge allowed opposing interpretations of Islam to spread, and the state was no longer seen to have the power to legitimate political or religious ideologies.

In Kenya, some of the same political dynamics occurred as in Indonesia, but the role of religious groups was different. In the African nation, as authoritarian leadership began to weaken in the late twentieth century, both

Islamic and Christian organizations supported efforts toward greater democracy, mobilizing their respective constituencies around the promise of a future not decided by the traditional leadership. Whereas in Indonesia, the flourishing democracy led to the diversity of religious voices in politics, in Kenya, both Islamic and Christian religious institutions took a step back from engaging in politics, according to a seminar participant, Robert Dowd, founding director of Notre Dame's Ford Family Program, which is actively involved in East Africa. Dowd reported on a discussion with a Kenyan Catholic bishop, who told him that once political parties were firmly established, the church could leave the public arena. According to the Kenyan bishop, "We don't need to be as involved as we once were," since it was now "the role of political parties to mobilize people."[11] The religious authorities were willing to step in to support wide political change but had less interest in supplanting the political government themselves. Their efforts were aimed at correcting the system, not becoming the system. But elsewhere in Africa, Christian activists have ignored the advice of the official church and mounted their own religious political struggles.

In the political instability that rose at the end of the twentieth century, with the dawn of the global era, secular leaders have recruited religious ideologies and leaders to their side, hoping that the legitimacy of religion would shore up their flagging power. In Egypt, for example, secular leaders have tried, and sometimes failed, in trying to gain religious support. Both Gamal Abdel Nasser and Anwar el-Sadat sought to gain favor with the influential Muslim Brotherhood in the twentieth century, a group that is still in a turbulent relationship with the Egyptian state, and then turned against it. Assassinations ensued on both sides, and a competition for power emerged that could be seen to be persisting even in the 2012 election of Mohammed Morsi and his subsequent removal from power. Egypt provides lurid proof that trying to please everyone can result in being seen as a traitor to both sides.

As the cracks began to show in the ability of the nation-state to provide solutions for the issues of the global era, new voices began to emerge from those spaces. By and large, those voices were based on a common value of individual human dignity. They carried a passion for democracy, though sometimes the tone of their critiques verged on anarchy. Computer hacking undertaken by the secretive movement Anonymous has been carried out with a pretension of citizen power. The revelation of secret U.S. government documents in 2013 by a government contract employee, Edward Snowden, was cheered by many around the world not only because he embarrassed Washington leaders but also because he showed the power of individuals to counter the most powerful agencies in the world. The same new communications technologies that enabled regimes to control information could be used to expose surveillance activities and share them around the world. The newly acquired ability for individuals and groups to effect change has been welcomed by most people, though it is often accompanied by a general distrust of institutional authorities.

Anarchy has been at the edge of many social movements in history, of course, and is not unique to the current situation. Most of the movements that captured the world's imagination in the beginning of the twenty-first century contained a more or less vocal contingent that sought the utter destruction of traditional power structures. Some of these groups formed around a kind of identity that might seem to have nothing to do with politics, such as soccer or music enthusiasm. During the revolutionary protests in Egypt following Arab Spring, bands of soccer fans played a critical role, helping to create an antiauthoritarian momentum without advocating a specific form of alternative government. While supporting a soccer team may seem like an unlikely basis for mobilization, it's also true that in some cultures, sports fanaticism is akin to religious zeal, and soccer teams can command as much loyalty as a state. Moreover, many soccer clubs are based at a particular locale, and groups supporting the same team have shared experiences that unite them, and they possess a common antipathy to the police and other authorities who try to control them. Like the Egyptian soccer fans, mass movements around the world often have had an antiauthoritarian character.

The Occupy Wall Street movement in the United States in 2011 to 2012 was, by nature, antiauthoritarian, since it challenged the corporate power structure of American society. Although most of the protestors who encamped in Zuccotti Park in New York's lower Manhattan financial district were peacefully protesting corporate privilege in the United States and the control of the "1 percent" over American politics, there was an anarchic strand to the protests as well. As the movement spread to most major American cities and abroad, the message of protest against government corruption and corporate control was tinged with a distrust of all established authoritarian institutions.

In Ukraine, in November 2013, protestors occupied Independence Square—popularly known simply as the *Maidan* (square)—in the heart of the capital city of Kiev. The protests precipitated a wider movement against the regime of the Russian-supported president, Viktor Yanukovych, which led to his ouster some months later, and they ignited a conflict between the new leaders of Ukraine and Russia's Vladimir Putin. Though most of the protestors were simply concerned about keeping Ukraine within the orbit of the European Union rather than joining Russia's hegemonic network of kindred states, the black-flag bearing ultranationalists in the protest square were, as Russian commentators were quick to point out, representatives of both anarchic and fascist aspects of Europe's recent past.

This antiauthoritarian current within contemporary global politics has spawned new groups of cowboy activists, but it has also transformed more established political organizations, including those associated with religion. In Iran, the election of Hassan Rouhani as president in 2013 was credited to a populist democratic movement that had earlier been a part of the Green Revolution to oust former President Mahmoud Ahmadinejad. In 2011, in the Tibetan government in exile, the Dalai Lama relinquished his political position at the head of the Tibetan community in favor of a democratically elected administration. He was said to have been inspired by democratic movements like those during Arab Spring, but it might also have been seen as an attempt to appease the Chinese government, which regarded him as a separatist political agitator. The Dalai Lama's decision divided the spiritual leadership from the political for the first time in over two hundred years in Tibet.

This antiauthoritarian and populist theme has become part of the culture of globalization and affects all institutions, including religious ones. In Protestant Christianity, new sects associated with evangelical populist movements have flourished while established liberal denominations such as Presbyterians and Methodists have dwindled in numbers. The Roman Catholic Church has also had trouble sustaining its numbers, and the popularity of Pope Francis, installed in 2013, has largely been due to the perception that he challenges the stuffy authoritarianism associated with his predecessor, Pope Benedict XVI, and much of the Catholic hierarchy in general. The American political scientist Susanne Rudolph has noted that popular religions, those she described as "from below," have been consistently surpassing those "from above."[12] The latter, exemplified by institutions like the Catholic Church, have fallen out of favor with many. Popular religions, with the ability for adherents to have a more direct role in their own salvation, have eclipsed those that dictate their paths to spiritual success for them.

Part of the reason for the decline in the popularity of the established Christian church is its traditional liaison with the political status quo. In

Latin America, for instance, the Catholic Church was aligned with colonial powers, and even after independence, church leaders were hand in glove with the new political leadership. The discussions in our seminar confirmed, however, that the church leaders no longer have the kind of influence that they had in the past. In Argentina, for instance, most citizens remember that the church was an ally and accomplice of the brutal military dictator Augusto Pinochet. In a post-Pinochet society, the church did not have the same influence to bend government policies in its direction. Despite the efforts of the former archbishop of Buenos Aires, Jorge Mario Bergoglio—the name Pope Francis enjoyed before being elevated to cardinal of Rome—Argentina ignored the church's pleas to reject government support for birth control and equal rights for gay people, including the official recognition of same-sex marriage. Though church officials opposed these liberal actions, the majority of Argentinians—regardless of their Catholic faith—accepted them.[13] Like religious people everywhere in the global age, Argentinian Catholics tended to be critical of authorities and to pick and choose what to accept as right.

In a global age in which it is not clear who is in charge and to whom one should be accountable, religious leadership evokes contradictory responses. On the one hand, it can be identified with the status quo and a support of the old style of secular nationalism. On the other hand, it can be seen as antiauthoritarian and revolutionary, a challenging new authority that is worthy of respect. In the Middle East, televised Muslim preachers have proclaimed a personal Islam that undercuts the authority of traditional imams, and Muslim political movements have often ignored the clerical establishment (except in Iran, where the clerical establishment has led the revolution). In the United States, one of the hallmarks of the religiosity of the extreme political right is its evangelistic anticlericalism. The authority of new religious voices seem to be compelling precisely because they challenge the old order and proclaim a new kind of personal truth.

The rebellious challenges to traditional social order in the global era have created the occasion for strident new religious voices as well. When Egypt's dictatorial president, Hosni Mubarak, was toppled during Arab Spring, a host of religiously related political groups emerged to claim the reins of power, including the long-banned Muslim Brotherhood and the rigid, Saudi-influenced Muslim Salafists, who previously had avoided government and instead stressed the people's responsibilities to God. According to a participant in our Cairo seminar, Saad Eddin Ibrahim, founder of the Ibn Khaldun Center for Development Studies in Cairo, when the Mubarak regime was toppled in 2011, the time was right for this devout cadre to seek power through the state, hence they formed their own al Nour political party.[14]

As for the democratic surge symbolized by Arab Spring, it knocked down the institutions that had dominated the public square for decades, leaving room for a multitude of new voices to be heard. Many of those voices belonged to heralds of the new cosmopolitan order, people celebrating a newfound borderless terrain and welcoming the new age. Others shouted for retreat into old identities and insulation from the global processes that unsettled them. In both cases, leadership identified with religion provided a locus of accountability, a trusted authority, and a harbor of certainty in a time of storms.

WANTING TO BE SECURE

This brings us to the third concern in an era of globalization, the longing for security. At the end of World War II, when the United Nations was created, the world was partitioned into neat little definable nation-states. Each nation provided a measure of domestic security to its people, and the whole international order was thought to create a tapestry of national security for which the administrative infrastructure of the United Nations provided an arena of rationality. Differences between countries could be settled in a parliamentary fashion.

It never really worked that way, of course. The United Nations proved to be a weak transgovernmental structure, a debating club for national representatives rather than a negotiating arena. More important, there were new forces in the latter half of the twentieth century that challenged the notion of individual national sovereignty. Those forces were related to the ideology of communism, the idea that state socialism could provide the basis for a transnational global order.

The specter of global communism terrified leaders of democratic capitalist nations, and as an iron curtain descended on Europe, a Cold War chilled the world. It divided Europe and Asia, sometimes literally tearing apart nations, as a wall separated West Germany from East Germany and a demilitarized zone divided North Korea from its neighbor in the south. More important were the global divisions between peoples and the imagined fears of conquest from either side. At our Moscow seminar, we were surprised to see that old Russians remembered a time during the Cold War when they were as afraid of Americans as we were of them. They imagined, as did we, that conquering hordes from the other side would roll over the borders, enslave their populations, and threaten their very lives.

In 1989 the Berlin wall came down, and the Cold War came to an end. Pundits such as Francis Fukuyama proclaimed "the end of history" and the termination of global ideological conflict.[15] It seemed, for a time, that secular nationalism had won. And yet the last decade of the twentieth century and the first decades of the twenty-first inherited mass disillusionment with the system of sovereign, secular nation-states. National unities were challenged by divisions based on religious and tribal identities, and new ideologies of nationalism emerged based on the sectarian interests of religion. Secular nationalism was found to be empty of the kind of guiding morality that religion had long provided for states, and new processes of globalization eroded the sovereignty of the nation-state itself.

In the global era, new threats to security emerged. Religious ideologies and organizations were seen as both the cause of insecurity and the antidote for it. Religion was both frightening and calming, though not necessarily at the same time.

Religion became frightening when it became linked with political violence, and in some extreme instances, with acts of terrorism. According to statistics kept by the U.S. State Department, religion has been associated with more instances of public violence in the last thirty years than at any time in the last two hundred years. More acts of political violence are associated with religious ideologies than secular ones, such as socialism or anarchic ideas. Before 1990 the major threat to world security was thought, in the West, to be the ideology of communism. In the decades since then—especially since the 9/11 attacks on the Pentagon and the World Trade Center in 2001—the major threat to world security has been perceived as religious extremism.

Elsewhere in this book we talk about how the rise of religious extremism is related to globalization—how the weakening of the nation-state in the global era has allowed the provincial forces of ethnicity and religious community to assert themselves as the basis of social order.[16] But there are other ways in which globalization has led more directly to a sense of social insecurity.

Globalization has disrupted the social fabric that helps individuals define themselves and assess their social roles. Let us assume that most people want to fit in with everyone else, follow the accepted norms, and do the right thing. In more stable societies, before the advent of the global era, all of the cultural cues of society reinforced one another. The teachings of a Muslim imam, for example, were consistent with images on a traditional Muslim society's television channels and with statements from its public authorities.

But in a global era, we are all bombarded with competing images of how to behave and succeed, even with competing images of what is the social good. In the Middle East, one of the most popular television programs is the old American situation comedy *Friends,* which projects the casual lifestyle of a group of unmarried young urban Americans. Global communications media portray one standard of acceptable social order, traditional religious teachers advocate a quite different one, and secular authorities might demand yet another set of social and public expectations. The shifts of the twenty-first century have upended traditional structures of authority, relocating centers of power and allowing a flood of perspectives on what "the good" is. Changes like this can be frightening, separating people from ways of life with which they were at least familiar, even if they did not directly benefit from them. These shifts have unanchored lives, challenging the structures that guided peoples' actions up to the present.

People exist in communities with particular rules—rules for behavior, rules of how to act in certain social positions, rules about what one can expect from appropriate behavior. These are generally implicit, taken for granted, without being plainly enumerated. We simply learn how to exist within the networks of our society by trial and error, following the models of others and having a general understanding of what Pierre Bourdieu called the *field* of our society.[17] The field is made of people and hierarchies, power and order, and we learn how to operate in the field by living in it. In our familiar world, we know instinctively who deserves respect, who wields authority in what areas, and how one can best navigate within the institutions of power. But in a time of rapid social change and competing images of public behavior, these networks are erased or shifted to a degree that they become unrecognizable.

Such a confusing state of affairs exists in many areas around the globe, with each context bringing its own particular constellation of power relations to the table. The new ideas of identity and conceptions of an expansive world that have found voice with the new global shift all shout for recognition, and the common citizen can be left in a quandary about which way to go. Ways of life that were taken for granted are smashed down, leaving people wondering what to do, whom to trust, and who they themselves are. The social and cultural changes in the twenty-first century occur at near light speed compared to similar changes in earlier world history.

In the global era, people have barely enough time to adjust to the new state of affairs before it changes again. This frantic pace has unsettled people to such an extent that they yearn for agents of constancy to provide an oasis in the shifting sands of today. Religious ideas, authorities, and communities appear as harbors in a storm. They are recognized, trusted institutions that have their bases of legitimacy in the divine order of the universe.

Still, stability can come at a cost. Religious leaders now struggle to come to terms with the very social landscape that the secular state was meant to address, namely the vast variation of identities housed within the borders of a nation. In places where nationalism looks toward religion for its identity, a sense of certainty may be provided by promoting one particular religious identity or interpretation above all others. As a result, those of another faith could be threatened with losing their standing within the national community or, worse, seeing legislation aimed at their groups specifically. As will be discussed more in the next chapter, when traditional religion wields state power, it often threatens those citizens who are not religious colleagues of the ruling group.

Religion is not only one thing. It is a repository of symbols, a system of belief, a conveyor of cultural rites, a structure of morality, an institution of power, and many other things as well. The perceived antiquity of its traditions appears to be constant over time, which gives people a sense of calm and reliable steadiness in a time of confusion and disruption. Today's global era is experiencing those dark moments, and in the tumult religion shines like a beacon of hope and reliability. However, just as religion is not one thing, it is not consistent over time. Just as any other institution changes, the social aspects of religion move in conjunction with flows of ideas and shifts in knowledge. Today's religious traditions are no exception and have been affected by the upheavals of globalization just as all other aspects of public life have been touched by global changes. Just how religion has been affected in the global era is the subject to which we now turn.

Devotee at the Sikh Golden Temple in Amritsar, India. Photograph by Mark Juergensmeyer.

TWO

Religion Tumbles and Turns

HOW RELIGION HAS BEEN AFFECTED
BY GLOBAL FORCES

PICTURE A ROOM FULL OF some of India's most influential scholars and religious leaders, the air charged with intellectual discussion on the changing role of religion in modern society; an overworked air conditioner hums in the background. The group at our Delhi workshop is sitting around tables configured in a circle, tables cluttered with water bottles and empty tea cups, and from time to time scholars seize the moment to click the "on" light on their microphones to announce that they have the floor. Most of the women are wearing stylish adaptations of traditional Indian saris and Punjabi dress; the men are in suits or white shirts and trousers. Aside from the fact that a few of the men are wearing the distinctive Sikh turban and some of them are sporting the sort of nationalist Indian vest associated with the Nehru years, most of them could be wearing the same outfits at an academic seminar anywhere in the world.

One of the men, however, stands out. He is wearing a kind of orange robe, a sheet really, gathered around his shoulders. On his forehead are two vertical white lines that are joined between his eyes. The marking signifies that he is a Vaishnava, a devotee of the avatars of Vishnu: Rama and Krishna. This sole holy man in the group is Shrivatsa Goswami, a Brahman priest, and he is not just any priest but the leader of one of the most important Vaishnava religious lineages in North India. He is also a scholar and was, for a time, the Hindu leader in residence at Harvard's Center for the Study of World Religion. He is often called upon to be the representative of Hinduism in international convocations, including a recent gathering at the United Nations.

But today Goswami is not talking about the power and influence of his own position or his own movement. He is discussing the remarkable growth of new religious movements in the subcontinent. These are movements that, in a broad sense, are part of Hinduism, but they are not under the jurisdiction of any of the traditional leaders or their authorities. The new movements include the Sathya Sai Baba movement based at Puttaparthi in Andhra Pradesh, in South India. When the movement's leader, Sathya Sai Baba, died in 2011, it was said that half a million devotees attended his memorial service. The Swaminarayan movement, based in the western Indian region of Gujarat, has a huge following among urban Indians and expatriate Indians living abroad in New York, London, Atlanta, and elsewhere. In all these places, the movement has erected enormous marble temples. One that was opened in Princeton, New Jersey, in 2014 is the size of a shopping mall. The numbers of devotees are in the millions. Several hundred thousand of followers flock to the festival events of another new religious group, the Radhasoami movement, which has created ideal cities near Agra and Amritsar in North India and whose living gurus are magnets for millions.

In describing these new movements, Shrivatsa Goswami was dispassionate, though one had to wonder if he felt a certain mixture of wonder and envy at the popularity of these new forms of Hinduism. In truth, he has no reason to be concerned, since his position as the inherited leader is secure, and his family leadership has a sizable following. The crowds gather eagerly in his small temple in the heart of the pilgrimage center of Vrindavan, said to be the childhood home of Lord Krishna, where he is much revered. Several hundred of the faithful will crowd noisily into the small space, the air thick with incense and the smell of candles. The devotees bend in reverence both to the images of the gods and to the priests themselves, including Goswami and his sons, naked from their waists up and garbed in baggy orange cloths, who hand out garlands of flowers and the sweet, sticky *prasad,* a blessed mixture of honey and ground meal. But the numbers in his reverent group pales by comparison with the sheer magnitude of followers of the new movements, especially in India's urban centers, where they appeal to a mobile middle class, a group whose size is truly impressive.

The explosion of membership in these new religious groups appears to be symptomatic of the challenges posed by the new shape of the global world. With the unstable boundaries of identity and increased interconnection between people, religion is often seen to offer stability amid the shifting sands. Even religious movements that are considered "new" locate themselves in relation to ancient traditions based in the cultural makeup of the populace. People taking part in these new movements can find a sense of community, a trusted authority, and meaning for their lives within the bounds of religion, all of which are linked to traditions anchored in the past.

At the same time, religion itself is changing in the face of global currents. Beliefs about the divine order are challenged by science, religious clerics are faced with opposition to their authority by secular leaders, and the link between religion and other identity markers such as ethnicity has been undermined by the demographic shifts of population. These and other changes in the modern world have forced religion to adapt. The situation of the liberal Protestant churches in twentieth-century America is a good example of these shifts, as the mainstream denominations that at one time were considered the backbone to America's middle class and a bulwark to what Robert Bellah called "civil religion" in America have seen a sharp decline in membership and attendance in the last century.[1]

It is important to note that a decrease in certain kinds of religiosity is not necessarily a decrease in spirituality. The numbers of people identifying as "less religious" has spiked in recent years, and in questionnaires people increasingly choose "none" when asked to name their religious preference, indicating that they are against not spirituality but institutional religion. The rise of what have come to be called the "nones" in Western nations is paralleled by a surge in religious adherence elsewhere. Religious belief used to be measured by how many people filled the pews, but today's religiosity doesn't admit to such simple measurements.

That said, huge megachurches have sprung up in many countries, founded by charismatic preachers like Joel Osteen in America or David Yonggi Cho in South Korea. Osteen's Lakewood Church in Texas is the largest congregation in the United States, boasting a regular attendance of nearly fifty thousand believers; that impressive number is dwarfed by Cho's Yoido Full Gospel Church, which vaunts a staggering membership of over a million Christians in Seoul. (Cho was forced to preach to a smaller crowd for a while, however, as he was convicted of embezzling $12 million from his parishioners in 2014 and sentenced to three years in prison.) At a time when many religious communities around the world are diminishing, when the dire predictions of religion's demise by secularist philosophers of the Enlightenment seems to be coming true in places like Europe, where church attendance is at a historic low, the global rise of these enormous megachurches and megacongregations is a testament to the continuing vitality of religion. They illustrate how the spiritual needs of people may vary during uncertain times, but religious institutions can and do adapt to the new world and avoid marginalization or decreased influence.

One enduring aspect of the Enlightenment's creation of the idea of religion, as we noted in the previous chapter, was the privatization of spirituality. Religious ideas and practices were regarded as having their proper place solely in the realm of the individual. This European notion of religion has influenced the urban culture of societies around the world, including those in traditional Muslim, Hindu, and Buddhist regions, where religion is usually seen as a seamless part of the society and culture. In urban India, according to Father John Chathanatt of the India Social Institute, who participated in our Delhi workshop, "religion has been sidelined into a private act."[2] In such settings, the privatization of belief has led to an emphasis on the emotional side of religion, especially by politicians seeking to mobilize religious doctrines and sentiments toward their political ends. By appealing to religion as a cultural sentiment rather than as an organization or structure of beliefs, the authority of traditional religious leaders is undercut. Consequently, new religious voices are speaking out and gaining influence, joining other antiauthoritarian trends of the global age.

RELIGION GONE WILD

Even in Vrindavan, the pilgrimage city thought to be the birthplace of Lord Krishna, where Shrivatsa Goswami presides over his ancient, family-run temple, Radha Raman, the religious landscape is changing. Just a few miles from where Goswami hands out flowers and honeyed *prasad* to his followers and leads the traditional Vaishnava rites, new temples have been constructed. These are ostensibly in honor of Lord Krishna, but they also venerate their wealthy mortal donors, who provided the funds and whose names are as associated with the Hindu deities in the minds of the masses who worship at the imposing new edifices.

Among these new temples is one that houses the tomb of Swami Bhaktivedanta Prabhupada, the leader of the International Society of Krishna Consciousness. A businessman from Calcutta, he travelled to Europe and United States in the 1960s and 1970s to propagate Krishna consciousness to young European and American devotees. Popularly known as the Hare Krishna Movement, an international community of followers of ISKCON today converges on the temple to Krishna that was built in the Swami's honor and spills over from the temple grounds into the narrow lanes of the village of Vrindavan. It is striking to see Caucasian faces peering from above orange robes at tea stalls, on bicycle rickshaws, and in the local shops. These Western followers of Hare Krishna are symbols of a new Hinduism that is both populist and global.

As the new temples in Vrindavan indicate, in the global era, conventional religious leaders and their organizations have come under siege from new movements unconcerned with, or even explicitly hostile to, the old guard. The glut of new religious movements in India has parallels in other parts of the world, where changing global dynamics have opened a space for dissenting voices. Some of these have openly engaged with the political process, seeking to effect change by directing policy. Others have turned to violence in their attempt to force the world to align with their vision of reality. However these new religious movements choose to engage, what unites them is their creation of different centers of authority, new avenues for identity, and new modes of belonging—all outside the control of the established religious authorities.

The new movements in India are neither violent nor especially political. What they are is unaccountable to traditional authorities, with the potential to become anything they want. Some leaders of the new movements have been accused of embezzlement and sexual abuse, but on the whole, the movements in India are harmless. For instance, the Sathya Sai Baba movement, a spiritual organization based around the teachings of the eponymous Indian guru, stresses the oneness of all beings and devotes itself to humanitarian projects. Education, medical-care projects, clean drinking water, and aid for victims of natural disasters are its stated focus. Such projects do not aim to directly shift public policy but to provide humanitarian assistance to those in need, followers and non-followers alike. It is true that there are tax incentives from the Indian government to provide social services, but it also is true that the philosophy of many of these movements include a devotion to *seva,* "service," a term that is applied both to serving the needs of the spiritual masters of the movements as well as serving the population as a whole. Many of the new religious movements surging throughout the world have widened their focus from solely spiritual aims to projects done in the service of a community that goes beyond the religious group.

This is the case in Japan, which has witnessed a remarkable eruption of new religious movements in the last few decades. Some of those movements have been bizarre—members of the PanaWave movement, for example, wear white gear to protect themselves from hidden electromagnetic rays that they imagine are harming people and bringing about the end of the world. But none of the new movements seemed especially dangerous until the Aum Shinrikyo movement's attack on the Tokyo subway in 1995. The movement was founded in 1984, developed out of a blend of Japanese and Indian forms of Buddhism, and it took on an extreme eschatological character under the guidance of Shoko Asahara, its leader. In March of 1995, members of the group released deadly sarin gas into the Tokyo subway during rush hour, killing twelve and injuring thousands. This attack was inspired by Asahara's belief that a cataclysmic event he called Armageddon would destroy the unworthy and leave only the righteous members of Aum Shinrikyo.

The group did not start out advocating terrorism, of course. It was a religious movement fully engaged with the modern world. But the confrontation turned deadly in a distinctly contemporary way. Not only did it make use of a vicious gas invented through advanced chemical processes, but it also propagated the prophecies of Asahara that were related to recent history. He envisioned a third world war at the beginning of the third millennium, one that would dwarf World War II in its destruction (a fearful claim in a country that had suffered the world's only atomic attacks). Moreover, he prophesized that the government of Japan would both perpetrate the attacks that would initiate the end times and ultimately fail to protect the Japanese population from the disasters that would occur. Asahara challenged the authority of the secular Japanese government by incorporating the fears of the late twentieth century and its technologies into prophecies that the nerve-gas attacks were meant to confirm.

The tragic loss of life of the sarin gas attacks was a calculated event. Asahara had conjured up an apocalyptic fantasy of the future, and the attack in the subways gave his prophecies credibility—to his followers, it seemed that Armageddon had begun and his prophecies were becoming real. After the attack, Japan went through a public and collective soul-searching, trying to understand how such a thing could happen. Many of the accusations pointed to the social crises that lay behind the creation of many of the new religions. People in Japan, like those in many industrialized nations, were experiencing an increased feeling of alienation and loss of dignity in the fast pace of urban life. Breaking from traditional cultures made this new life possible, but it also unanchored people from the structures of meaning that made sense of the world around them. New religious movements such as Aum Shinrikyo blended a prophetic vision and a charismatic leader with the promise of inner peace and personal transformation. It was a heady combination. While the Aum Shinrikyo vision of the world was a violent one, many other new religious movements, as well as many traditional religions, blended the idea of a knowable future (often a dangerous one) with the individual's ability to become something more than merely ordinary. The differences among the new movements and religions lay in the shape of that future, the practices required to achieve personal enlightenment, and the perception of what the world needed in order to be transformed.

In the People's Republic of China (PRC), religious movements have long been seen as a threat to the atheist state. At least since the Communist Revolution under Chairman Mao Zedong, religion has been charged with stunting progress and stealing loyalty away from its proper place: Chinese nationalism and the Communist Party. A fear of religion has occurred in other cultures as well, of course—during the campaign of John F. Kennedy for the presidency of the United States, for example, fears were rife that his Catholicism meant that his loyalty was ultimately to the pope, who would therefore be able to dictate U.S. policy. In China, however, any kind of religion was regarded as potentially dangerous to public life. For that reason, it has been carefully controlled. Article 36 of China's constitution expressly defends freedom of religion, but only those religions sanctioned by the government and controlled by it. In China there are only five official religions—Buddhism, Taoism, Islam, Catholicism, and Protestantism—and their actions are carefully monitored by government watchdogs. Any religious group unaffiliated with the approved versions of these faiths does not enjoy legal protection, and at times, these groups have suffered legal repression.

Such is the case with the religious movement known as Falun Gong (or Falun Dafa), which has been under government scrutiny at least since their large-scale protest on April 25, 1999, when more than ten thousand adherents gathered to seek governmental recognition for their movement. Their demands were ignored, and the group was banned only a few months later. Since then, the persecution of the movement has persisted. Though Chinese state officials are rumored to have been part of the group in the early 1990s, thousands of people associated with Falun Gong have been detained since the protest, and many have died in Chinese custody.

Falun Gong is a syncretic spiritual system that blends aspects of Buddhism, forms of mysticism, and qigong (a kind of martial-arts training similar to tai chi, sometimes called "shadow-boxing"). The movement has repeatedly stressed that it seeks only legal recognition for its practices, not political power. Still, the PRC has condemned the group as an enemy of the state. What frightened the Chinese officials were two things: it is not controlled by the government, and its effortless ability to mobilize huge numbers of members in protest rallies. If it can gather such impressive crowds so quickly, the officials reasoned, it could threaten government itself if it chose to do so. Their sheer potential political power, therefore, made them scary.

In Hong Kong, which allows freedom of speech, even though it is controlled by the government of China, adherents of Falun Gong have been able to voice their anger against what they regard as a Chinese government pogrom against their movement. At the entrance to the Star Ferry, which plies between Hong Kong Island and the peninsula of Kowloon, posters vividly display what the Falun Gong supporters state are savage attacks on their members by the Chinese police. Clearly, the urban, educated, and middle-class supporters of the Falun Gong movement have not been afraid to speak out against its opponents when they have the chance. They have publicized the Chinese government's discrimination against their movement around the world. Needless to say, this has not helped the politics-free image of an organization sometimes described as an "exercise group." But the worldwide support has shed light on the treatment of Falun Gong practitioners, further calling into question the Chinese government's already spotty record on human rights.

Criticisms of China's human-rights record have regularly appeared in global media, but perhaps ironically, China has based their charges against the group on the same ground. Chinese officials contend that Falun Gong's beliefs cause its practitioners to rely too much on meditation and paranormal methods of healing instead of modern medicine. It has also claimed that the group has hijacked state-run satellite signals and even murdered vagrants in order to achieve some sort of ideal spiritual state.[3] The state's efforts have resulted in the removal of many of the movement's spiritual leaders and have forced adherents to move their practices underground. Its charismatic leader in exile, Li Hongzhi, often referred to simply as "Him," continues to attract devotees to his particular brand of spirituality blended with exercise, and the group's numbers have swollen in spite of the PRC's ban. The ban itself has been interpreted by Hongzhi as a test from heaven to be endured, and the government's actions have been read as acts in a kind of apocalyptic scenario.[4] Tensions continue between the movement and the Chinese government and vividly portray how a new religious movement with global connections can become politically potent and challenge the authority of nation-states.

The rise of new Islamic religious movements and figures has presented a global political challenge as well. The use of television and the internet to convey religious thoughts and practices has proven very effective in the Middle East, where charismatic personalities challenge traditional religious authorities by directly addressing large numbers of people not only in mosques and in the streets but also in the living rooms of private homes. The model is well known in Western nations, especially in the United States, where demagogues such as Pat Robertson and Jerry Falwell are household names. Televangelists can spread their message beyond the walls of both church and mosque. The voices of Muslim televangelism in the Middle East speak to all places along the spectrum—conservative, liberal, and moderate—and their popularity has the potential to change the religious discussion without recourse to conventional religious officials. No longer do spiritual teachers require a brick-and-mortar building; their temples are satellites and the internet, and the new breed of preachers has harnessed these democratic medium to great effect.

Perhaps no televangelist in the Middle East has proven more effective than Amr Khaled, an Egyptian who was ranked by Time Magazine in 2007 as the thirteenth most influential person in the world. A former accountant, Khaled's particular brand of preaching stresses an understanding of Islam that is tolerant and open, and promotes cross-cultural understanding as well as harmony with the West. He has explicitly attacked the mindsets of ultra-conservatives and Salafi Islamic extremism, emphasizing instead the ability for Muslims to be modern, successful, and religious with no contradiction. This approach has won him an enormous audience across the Middle East and North Africa, especially in urban areas. His television shows are especially popular in places that have experienced a loss of local traditions and customs, where individuals are searching for a new way to be Muslim outside the rituals and doctrines of their parents. Khaled's preaching has filled that vacuum, and his message has spread farther than previously would have been possible.

Khaled himself is both an agent and product of global processes. Fluent in English, he uses an Egyptian vernacular in his programs as opposed to the formal, classical Arabic favored by the more traditional Islamic leaders. This choice decreases the distance between him and his viewers and merges with the general populist trend across the world. His shows are produced by multinational companies, which provided the funds for him to continue preaching after he was banned from television in his home country. The increased connectivity made possible by satellite and internet technologies has thwarted any possibility for traditional religious and political leaders to control Khaled's message. Those technologies have also allowed Khaled to reach and influence huge numbers of people across national boundaries.

The central message of Khaled's preaching is a focus on piety over politics, making him, theoretically, as apolitical as any other strictly religious organization, but of course, the same can be said of Falun Gong. Moreover, Khaled emphasizes the need to demonstrate one's piety in action, not mere words. This emphasis led to the development in 2010 of a television show that put a religious twist on the popular U.S. show *The Apprentice,* the brainchild of Donald Trump. The shows are as different as their creators, and Khaled's program, *Mujaddidun,* centers on using religious principles to inspire projects aimed at poor and troubled communities. Teams that do the least good in an episode are confronted with Amr Khaled telling them "you're fired."

Khaled's use of the boardroom format and catchphrase of Donald Trump's show is the only similarity between the two programs. *Mujaddidun* challenges young Muslims to create effective and sustainable programs to help those in need across the Arabic world.[5] The title of the show comes from an Arabic word meaning "reviver" or "renewer" and carries the sense of an agent who appears at the end of an era to revitalize Islam itself. This seems to be precisely what Khaled is aiming at: a vision of Islam that highlights care for community and activism rather than obeying strict Islamic rules for behavior—following what is approved (halal) or avoiding what is forbidden (haram).

Khaled's show has wide influence across national borders. It can focus on humanitarian aid for the poor in Amman, Jordan, and be watched by viewers in Sanaa, Yemen, and impact viewers' understanding of Islam in both locations. The emphasis on what is possible through faith has shown to be extremely popular with many young Muslims dissatisfied with traditional interpretations of religious doctrine. Khaled's ability to mobilize young believers, however, carries the potential of political power. Like the Falun Gong in China, Khaled's public influence is a concern by governments that are primarily concerned about their own self-preservation. This fear caused Hosni Mubarak's Egyptian government to terminate all of Khaled's projects in his native country after the start of the Arab Spring uprisings. But Khaled is not easily muzzled, and his iconic status has also spawned a wave of other new televangelists, such as Mostafa Hosni, whose show *Love Story* discusses issues of faith in the setting of a pop-music show.

Khaled's brand of religious television is not the only form of televangelism growing in popularity in the Middle East. The technologies that allow for voices like Khaled's also carry more conservative voices. One of the more well-known and vociferous Egyptian tele-preachers is Ahmed Abdallah, also known as Abu Islam. Abdallah made international headlines in 2012 when he tore a Christian Bible to shreds before the U.S. embassy in protest over the inflammatory film *Innocence of Muslims*. Produced by an Egyptian-American in California, *Innocence of Muslims* was a vicious attack on the Prophet Muhammad and his followers that sparked outrage when it was translated into Arabic and linked to the blog of the National American Coptic Assembly. Abdallah's protest was one of many that took place around the Middle East, and the film was initially thought to be the catalyst of the deadly attack on the U.S. embassy in Benghazi, Libya.

Like the Christian extremist, Florida pastor Terry Jones, whose public burning of a copy of the Qur'an was met with global fury, Abdallah's destruction of a copy of the Bible brought him a great deal of attention. He was previously well known for his hateful speeches about the Coptic Christian community, and his actions in front of the American embassy in Egypt were part of a demonstration driven mainly by the Salafis, Muslim extremists who are the main audience for Abdallah's sermons. Those sermons found a new home when Abdallah founded the Islamic satellite-television channel Al-Omma in 2012. In 2013, however, Abdallah was convicted on charges that he broke Egypt's anti-blasphemy laws, which declare it a crime to show contempt toward any of the "heavenly religions": Islam, Christianity, and Judaism. This was one of the few examples of the law's application to the contempt of a religion other than Islam.

Abdallah's conservative style of preaching has a complement in Khaled Abdullah (no relation to Ahmed Abdallah or to the moderate Muslim televangelist, Amr Khaled). Abdullah claims to be a sheik, and his Salafist message closely resembles that of his contemporary, Ahmed Abdallah. On his talk show, set in Egypt and broadcast on satellite-television channel Al-Nas, Abdullah also railed against *Innocence of Muslims* and blamed Coptic Christians for its creation and production. He spread that message at least as far as the estimated three hundred thousand viewers who visited his YouTube channel.

Abdullah's rants do not only fall upon the Copts, as much of the world finds its way into his preaching. He has accused secularists of being homosexual and Shi'ites of planning the downfall of Islam, and he has spit hatred against the West, the Jewish people, and the nations of Israel and Iran. On his program, he blamed the uprising in Egypt on foolish children who were being controlled by Western interests, and he spoke of the need of a return of the traditional moral values that are contained, he claims, only in the Salafi ideology.

These examples highlight the conflicting narratives playing out on satellite and internet television channels. On the one hand are those celebrities who might be said to be of the Facebook generation: liberal, secular, university educated, and led by the popular televangelist Amr Khaled. Traditional government and religious leaders find them threatening. On the other hand are the conservative, anti-Western Islamist voices. They have likewise been suppressed but still find internet and television outlets that allow them to reach a large transnational audience. And in the middle are the traditional religious institutions that for centuries have had a virtual monopoly on the religious communication to the masses. Their place as guardians of the faith have been bypassed by popular figures who have broken all the old institutional boundaries and no longer have any need for their custody or support.

POLITICS AND RELIGION IN AN INCENDIARY MIX

In general, there is nothing inherently threatening about the televangelists in Egypt, the Hare Krishnas in Vrindavan, or many of the other forms of popular, globalized religiosity around the world. But the same cannot be said for some of the other, more strident, and overtly political new transnational religious movements. In 2014, the extremist rebel movement in Syria that was for a time affiliated with al-Qaeda took on a new identity as the Islamic State of Iraq and Syria and went on a remarkable raid across the border into western Iraq, where it seized large swaths of territory, including Mosul, Iraq's second largest city, and some of the most important oil refineries in the country. Along with a rigid and uncompromising interpretation of shari'ah law, the vanguards of the movement used public beheadings as a way of advertising their savage determination. It then changed its name to the Islamic State, proclaiming that a new Muslim nation had been conceived, one that would eventually embrace the world.

In Egypt, violence in the name of religion again became a form of protest in the post–Arab Spring era. The rise of the Muslim Brotherhood as a democratically elected religio-political force was short-lived, as the military regime led by General Abdel Fattah al-Sisi toppled the government in 2013 in the midst of widespread protests against Morsi and the brotherhood. The complaint against the Muslim Brotherhood's regime was largely incompetence and favoritism, but many were also concerned about its extreme Islamic agenda. The return of the Bharatiya Janata Party in India in 2014 raised similar fears—that once a political party with a religious agenda comes to power, it will promote its own religious views.

The rise of religious politics is one of the peculiarities of the end of the twentieth century and the beginning of the twenty-first. But it is usually a religious politics that is promoted by laity, not the clerical leadership. Seldom have religious leaders and institutions become directly involved in the governance of their country. The theocracy of the Islamic Republic of Iran, a political system with its explicit basis in the religious authority of an ayatollah, is an anomaly in this regard.

In many other areas of the world, the religious influence on political life is more indirect, though often significant. In India, Indonesia, Bhutan, Myanmar, Israel, Pakistan, Saudi Arabia, and to some extent, the United States, movements with an extreme religious agenda have successfully pressured political leaders to adopt policies in line with their beliefs. In these cases, the politicians yielded to the religious movements in order to curry their favor and secure the support of their followers. In Indonesia, for instance, religious groups have encouraged the government to take a stand against movements that some Muslim leaders regard as heretical, such as Baha'i and Ahmadiyya. In Israel, the vision of Messianic Zionists for the creation of "biblical Israel" by incorporating the West Bank has made it difficult to negotiate a two-state solution for the Israel-Palestine conflict. In Myanmar, Bhutan, and Sri Lanka, Buddhist nationalists have pressured the governments to take positions that marginalize religious minorities. And in the United States, right-wing Christians have promoted public laws in line with their religious beliefs, especially regarding such matters as abortion rights and the rights of homosexuals.

Pakistan is an interesting example of how religion and politics have interacted virtually from the country's inception. The influence of religious groups on government policy is especially apparent in the education system. According to one of our workshop participants, I. A. Rehman, who was a founding member of the Pakistan-India Human Rights Commission, the government has been persuaded to incorporate religious teachings in schools, colleges, and universities "to the extent that if a student candidate for admission to a medical college secures 95 percent marks in medical-related subjects but fails in *islamiat* [Islamic studies], he cannot get admission into a medical college."[6] Such a strategy not only forces religious belief onto all members of the nation but also privileges Muslim believers. Even in careers as seemingly unconnected to religion as medicine, religion becomes essential.

The government of Indonesia, the world's largest Islamic country, has also been pressured by religious groups to adopt policies promoted by hardline Muslim leaders. The nation officially recognizes freedom of religious belief and practice (chapter 11 of the Indonesian Constitution), yet only Islam, Protestant and Catholic Christianity, Hinduism, Buddhism, and Confucianism are recognized as official religions. (It is interesting to compare this list with the People's Republic of China's roster of official religions, which neglects Hinduism and swaps Taoism for Confucianism, since the Chinese government regards Confucianism as a philosophy.)

While Indonesia's constitution guarantees freedom of religion, Islamic groups can and do exert influence on government policies, including the creation of a government-sanctioned blasphemy law aimed at small Islamic-related sects. The government law essentially endorsed a *fatwa* (religious injunction) issued in 2005 by the Indonesian Ulema Council (*Majelis Ulama Indonesia*—MUI) against the Ahmadiyya sect of Islam, declaring it heretical and outside the bounds of Islam. Ahmadiyya was founded in India at the end of the nineteenth century by Mirza Ghulam Ahmad, who blended in aspects of Christianity and was declared to be the second coming of Jesus and the long awaited Mahdi (the last imam, whose arrival foretells the end times). The group maintains a strong presence in over two hundred countries, and prophecies that Judaism, Zoroastrianism, Hinduism, Buddhism, Taoism, and other religious traditions will converge in the true Islamic doctrine.[7] Ahmadi Muslims, as the sect's followers are called, have come out categorically against the worldwide violence of jihadist Muslims, choosing instead to promote peace and a separation of state and religion. In many ways, Ahmadiyya exemplifies a modern, global religion. It reaches across borders, preaches peace and unity, and speaks out against violence of any sort.

It's therefore a tragic paradox that members of the movement have themselves been the target of violence. Three years after the MUI declared the group heretical, the Indonesian government took action against Ahmadi Muslims. In a 2008 letter, the Ministry of Religious Affairs, along with the Home Ministry, restricted the spread of Ahmadiyya within Indonesia, leading to some areas banning the faith altogether. Since then Ahmadis have suffered repeated persecution at the hands of government officials and ongoing bouts of violence at the hands of the populace. In February of 2011, three

Ahmadi Muslims were brutally murdered at the hands of a mob, and those identified as the perpetrators received only three to six months in prison. International outcry followed, from both states and international non-governmental organizations, but had little effect. In August 2014, however, when Joko Widodo was elected president of Indonesia, one of his first acts was to soften the government's stance toward minority Islamic-related communities such as Baha'i and Ahmadiyya.

In India, the resurgence of the Hindu-oriented Bharatiya Janata Party in the 2014 elections renewed fears of religious influence in government policies. For centuries, however, religion has been a feature of India's public life. The Hindu Vaishnava leader, Shrivatsa Goswami, who participated in our Delhi workshop, cited the experiences of his coreligionists in relation to state power at the time of the founding of his temple in the pilgrimage city of Vrindavan in the sixteenth century.[8] Goswami lauded the outcome of that dialogue, saying it brought about an area that excelled in economics, art, architecture, painting, music, dance, and other fields.[9]

Another participant in the Delhi workshop, Pralay Kanungo, a professor at the Center for Political Studies at Jawaharlal Nehru University's School of Social Sciences, agreed that there has always been a relationship between Indian political leaders and religion but was less optimistic about the results of that relationship today. In the twentieth century, the main issue in the discussion between religion and state power in India revolved around tax concessions for recognized Hindu organizations. Now, according to Kanungo, the focus has spread far beyond economic issues. Religious leaders have recognized how their power can influence the establishment of state policies favorable to their groups, including the procurement of land for religious universities and ashrams (spiritual refuges).

This new situation, placed in the context of the long history of religion and state power in India, led Kanungo to ask, "Who is using whom?" Earlier political leaders thought that they were using religion by going to religious sites, publicly praying, adopting the religious greeting "namaste," and making other acts and statements of piety to garner votes. But today, according to Kanungo, "the situation has been reversed."[10] Where politics and religion meet, a diversity of variables determine who will end on top. Even in nations with secular governments, religious groups can directly affect policies in many ways. That remains the case even in places where states are nominally secular and the separation of religious institutions and the state are constitutionally mandated.

But not all countries adhere to a strict separation of church (or similar religious institution) and state. Argentina provides an instance where the state's relationship with religion is codified in the constitution itself. It is important to recognize the role Western colonialism played in the development of the Argentine state, a project that was accomplished in concert with the Catholic Church. Part of the justification the sixteenth-century Spanish used for setting up colonies in Latin America was that they were attempting to missionize and convert the heathens, bringing them into the Christian faith. This explanation avoided the fact that they were also exploiting the indigenous people and their resources. The United States used a very similar religious cloak in its expansion west to the shores of the Pacific Ocean and trammeling of American Indian territory.[11]

When the Spanish colonization of Argentina ended in the early nineteenth century, rule by a foreign power was replaced with that of a local military dictatorship.[12] The role of the Catholic Church and its missionaries in the colonial era led to strong relations between the religious and civic authorities, which continued after independence; the Argentine Constitution reflects that connection. At our workshop in Buenos Aires, Leonor Slavsky, senior researcher at the National Institute of Anthropology, described how Catholicism was legally instituted as the favored religion of the country. Where the Argentine Constitution addressed the issue of indigenous minorities in the country, Slavsky noted that one article stated that "the mission of the National Congress is to keep peaceful relationships on the borders and to convert indigenous people to Catholicism."[13] Conversion, which provided a blind for the colonial project Argentina had only just shaken off, was reaffirmed for the self-governing state. This statute was linked with several other issues of religious favoritism, such as the requirement for all state officials to profess the Catholic faith, though this was eventually changed through legislative action. By the time the constitution was reformed in 1994, all that remained of this religious favoritism was the requirement that the president be Catholic.

The story of Argentina's relationship with the Catholic Church does not end here. The state's policies toward issues such as abortion and divorce have been heavily influenced by the church. According to Slavsky, however, "there is a difference between the intervention of the church on the political level and the church in everyday life."[14] Where the former may be strong in Argentina, Slavsky sees little attention paid to the church in the daily life of many Argentinians. And the influence on the state is waning as well. As we mentioned earlier, Pope Francis discovered this when he was a cardinal in Buenos Aires and pled with the government not to approve same-sex marriage—pleas that fell on deaf ears, as the marriages were approved in Argentina in 2010.

The state is not the only political actor that has had a relationship with religion. In recent decades, movements for social and political change have also had a religious character. A prominent example is the liberation theology movement that arose in the 1960s in Central and South America. It began as a response to the conditions of laborers and those on the periphery of society: indigenous people, *mestizos* (people descended from European and indigenous ancestry), and the rural and urban poor. Catholics who were moved by the plight of these groups began creating religious social programs and institutions, prompted by a radical new reading of Christian scripture. The focus was on social justice and the admonition of the Gospels to serve the poor.[15]

Liberation theology continued to gain support in Catholic circles throughout the 1970s and 1980s, finding champions in Bishop Samuel Ruiz and Archbishop Óscar Romero, both of whom are considered to be apostles of social change in Latin America. Marianne Loewe, director of Concern America, a humanitarian refugee-services organization, who participated in our workshop on Latin America and the Caribbean, noted that these two venerated figures were able to effect monumental transformations. Ruiz and Romero had an impact especially in the indigenous communities, even without the official support of Rome,[16] which in 1984 declared liberation theology to be a religious deviation, an ideology that employed Marxist concepts.

At that same workshop, Cecelia Lynch, director of the Center for Global Peace and Conflict Studies at UC Irvine, observed that the liberation theology movement was a precursor to the humanitarian efforts of modern international nongovernment organizations (NGOs). She saw the religious-political nexus of Latin American Catholic culture to be part of the spirit of recent humanitarian work in the region, even though it is conducted by organizations that do not necessarily regard themselves as religious. "There needs to be an awareness of intersecting landscapes—the landscape of religion and politics in Latin America and the landscape of the development of this field of humanitarianism ... and NGO work," Lynch explained.[17] Using the term *landscapes* captures the idea that there are peaks and valleys of connection between religion and the state in diverse contexts. According to Lynch, one of the contributions of the liberation theology movement was to clarify the connection between religion and politics in the Latin American scene.[18]

This connection is not specific to the global era, as there is a history of religious value systems being deployed in humanitarian projects. This is true throughout the world, in North Africa and the Middle East as well as in Latin America, as was pointed out by one of our Middle East workshop participants, Mohammed Bamyeh, a sociologist who is editor of the *International Sociology Review of Books*. Bamyeh spoke of religion's role in anticolonial projects in North Africa. According to him, Libya and especially Algeria were the two early theaters where Muslim Sufi orders were mobilized against Western colonialism. This kind of antistate Muslim activism was revived, according to Bamyeh, in the radical movements of the late twentieth century including jihadi movements associated with al-Qaeda.[19] Like waves on a beach, the force religion can exert ebbs and flows over time. Some of this religious antistate activism was replaced by more secular forms, according to Bamyeh.[20] Another participant in the Middle East workshop—Jeffrey Haynes, director of the Centre for the Study of Religion, Conflict and Cooperation at London Metropolitan University—pointed out that the experience in Iran was the opposite. There, a secular political movement initiated the Iranian Revolution in 1978 but was superseded by religious elements that gave the movement its distinct Shi'a religious character.[21]

In many places, it is not easy to make a sharp distinction between what is a religious and what is a secular political movement.[22] The Muslim Brotherhood (*al-Ikhwan al-Muslimun* in Arabic) is an example of this point. It was founded by Hassan al-Banna in Egypt in 1928 with the idea that political rule should be based on shari'ah, the moral and legal order founded on Islamic doctrine. It has been politically prominent ever since, alternatively celebrated for its morality and piety and decried as a treasonous usurper of power. Though it bears the name of Islam, it is largely a lay organization, led by businessmen, doctors, lawyers, and administrators. Some years ago, when one of the authors of this book was in Cairo and followed the address he was given for the offices of the Muslim Brotherhood, he was surprised to see that they shared space with the Medical Association of Egypt. Why? Because, he was told, so many of the leaders of the Muslim Brotherhood were doctors or otherwise associated with the medical profession. The official Muslim clergy in the country are usually not involved. As we mentioned earlier, when we met with the Grand Mufti of Egypt, the highest-ranking Muslim cleric in Egypt, who administers the official network of mosques and imams throughout the country, he expressed great reservations about whether clergy should be involved in the Muslim Brotherhood organization. The Mufti, Ali Gomaa, said that, in his opinion, religion and politics should be separate and that the Muslim Brotherhood did not represent the Muslim establishment in Egypt.

Despite its concentration of power into the hands of a few select men and a particularistic interpretation of Islam, the Brotherhood gained enough power to pose a threat first to the British-backed Egyptian monarchy and then, following the 1952 revolution, the Egyptian Republic. A member of the group was accused of the 1954 attempted assassination of Gamal Abdel Nasser, second president of the Egyptian Republic, following which it was disbanded. It continued to be politically active, however, and the independent members of Egypt's parliament who were sympathetic to the Muslim Brotherhood were often sufficient in numbers to constitute a rival political bloc to Egypt's ruling party.

During the Arab Spring, Egypt took center stage, even though the movement began in Tunisia on December 17, 2010, with the self-immolation of Mohammed Bouazizi. The massive protests in Cairo's Tahrir Square became the center of the Arab world and the focus of the world's attention. Some called it the "Twitter revolution," as the use of social media such as Twitter, Facebook, and YouTube helped the organizers of the rallies communicate with each other and with the wider world. Attempts by President Hosni Mubarak to turn off the internet were unsuccessful, since that act would have disrupted Egypt's business community as well as the protestors. Our own observation of similar rallies in Tahrir Square later that year confirmed that the protest gathering was a diverse group, largely young and educated and technologically sophisticated.

The Muslim Brotherhood was initially ambivalent about the protests. Though the Arab Spring movement was blessed by imams and other religious leaders, and some of the largest rallies took place after Friday prayers, the movement was not narrowly religious; nor was it sectarian. In an interesting moment during the early stages of the protest, when Mubarak's thugs were trying to disrupt the gathering, Egyptian Coptic Christians formed a protective circle around Muslims who were trying to conduct their daily prayers in the midst of the frenzy. Then on Sunday, when the Christians had their own worship circle, it was a ring of Muslims who guarded them so they could worship without interruption.

The events of Tahrir Square led to Egypt's first competitive presidential election, at the beginning of 2012. Sixteen months after the military removed Hosni Mubarak from power and promised continued progress toward democracy, the people elected Mohammed Morsi to the presidency. Morsi, a

U.S.-trained engineer and one-time Egyptian legislator, defeated a former general of the Egyptian Air Force. That a member of the military, who not only held power during the transition but also controlled the country's arsenal, lost the election raised international fears that Egypt's march toward democracy would be cut short by an army that would refuse to relinquish power. That prophecy turned out to be true. For a time, however, an Islamist democracy had been created in the land of the Nile. Though Morsi had studied at the University of Southern California and taught for a time at California State University at Fresno, he was perceived as being a new kind of Egyptian leader, one who was anti-Western and dedicated to Hassan al-Banna's notion of an Islamic state.

Though the rallies in Tahrir certainly seemed to support the idea of democracy, many of the young protestors had not dreamed that this democracy would lead to the establishment of an Islamic regime. Mohammed Bamyeh suggested the best label for the kind of Egyptian state desired by the protestors was not *religious,* though they wanted one based in a religious narrative. What they wanted, Bamyeh asserted, was "the idea of the civic state," which was "neither military nor religious."[23] According to Bamyeh, even young members of the Muslim Brotherhood were chanting for a civic state. He went on to say that a student affiliated with the Muslim theological center Al-Azhar defended the idea of the civic state by citing the prophet Muhammad as "the first person in history to establish a civic state, rather than a religious state."[24] Clearly these protestors were searching for a middle ground between their faith and their desire for a modern, democratic nation.

Not five months after being elected, however, Morsi and his fellows in the Muslim Brotherhood were already seeing their positions of power begin to erode. They attempted to counter the opposition by quickly passing a constitution (which was rejected by many parties), granting the president powers beyond what was considered acceptable for a democracy, and instilling what many thought amounted to martial law. None of it worked, and it succeeded only in strengthening the opposition and exacerbating the crisis. One year after taking power in Egypt's first democratic election, Mohammed Morsi was removed from power by the military and arrested. Understandably, supporters of Morsi in the Muslim Brotherhood denounced the move and refused to recognize the new government. They set up camps of opposition in public squares and nearby mosques, but their resistance was crushed, often brutally, with great loss of life.

The Muslim Brotherhood challenged the new elections called by Abdul Fattah al-Sisi, the former head of the Egyptian armed forces, in May 2014, and urged its followers to boycott the polls. As a result, the polls were kept open for three days in order to gain enough votes for the election to be deemed legitimate. The Muslim Brotherhood continue to demand that the dictates of Islam be at the core of any Egyptian nation and have declared that the revolution that began in 2011 continues today. They have also declared their intent to bring down al-Sisi for the good of Egypt.[25] The cycle of power struggles between the secularist Egyptian state, especially its military wing, and the Muslim Brotherhood have continued into the second decade of the twenty-first century.

In the previous chapter, we talked about how the dramatic social changes in the global era have upset the old national centers of power. The weakening of the nation-state, the emergence of transnational communities of identity and interaction, and the ability of modern technology to give voice to individuals and once-marginal elements of society have all challenged the national status quo. A new global antiauthoritarianism is in the works that, in its best moments, looks like democratic populism and, in its worst moments, looks like anarchy. In this chapter, we have seen how these same changes are shaking the foundations of the old religious establishments as well. Sometimes this antiauthoritarian religiosity has resulted in an explosion of violence, self-harm, and hatred. Other times, it has forged new concepts of communal support and administration. In yet other instances, it has joined forces with political leadership to attempt new forms of religious nationalism. It is not clear which, if any, of these alternatives to the traditional religious institutions will dominate, or indeed, if the expressions and organization of religion in the twenty-first century will ever look the same as they have in the past.

New Orthodox Cathedral, Moscow. Photograph by Mark Juergensmeyer.

THREE

Religion Resists and Soothes

RELIGIOUS RESPONSES TO GLOBALIZATION

IN MOSCOW, IT TOOK AN hour in congested traffic to get from our hotel to Lomonosov Moscow State University—just blocks away—where a gathering of scholars and religious officials had come together to discuss the profound changes that had occurred in Russia's religious society since the breakup of the Soviet Union in 1991. It wasn't just the traffic that symbolized the remarkable changes in Russian society in recent decades. Along with aggressive modern capitalism has emerged a renewed Russian nationalism. At the heart of it is religion, so it was appropriate that our gathering included representatives of Russia's leading religious communities.

Perhaps the most imposing figure in the group was Father Mikhail Zakharov, an archpriest in the Russian Orthodox Church, who wore a long beard, flowing black robes surmounted by a silver cross, and the elegant cylindrical black hat that is characteristic of Orthodox dress. He is a scholar in addition to being a cleric, a member of an institute for the study of religion and society, and was pursuing advanced scientific research in physics. But even more interesting was the fact that he had formerly been a member of the Communist Party. He had come to accept Marxism, he explained, because of his love of philosophy, and this same interest propelled him in the direction of theology and a leadership role in the church. When he left the party, he said, it was like "going through purgatory." But now, he affirmed, the church had been reaccepted into Russian society and was playing a major role in its social and cultural reconstruction.

This was exactly the point that interested us. Just how, we asked him, was the church playing this role, and how did it fit into post-Soviet Russian sensibilities?

Father Mikhail explained that the church had been closely associated with the monarchy and with Russian nationalism throughout history, so it was natural for the church to have a close relationship to power in the post-Soviet era. But, we wondered, doesn't this create a sense of marginalization among Muslims, Jews, Protestant and Catholic Christians, and others who are a part of a society in Russia, which—as in the rest of the world—is increasingly becoming multicultural?

"No, under no circumstances," Father Mikhail said, in a booming baritone. He went on to explain that in the history of Russia, there had been Muslim communities side by side with Russian Orthodox ones—the Tatar, for instance—and that relations were always congenial. He went on to insist that "there had never been any significant controversies" between the religious communities, and that, quite the opposite, the influence of the Orthodox leadership helped to make the official policies more tolerant by making them more sensitive to religious issues.

A representative of the Moscow Muslim community who was at the workshop hastened to confirm that his community was treated well, by and large, and that they appreciated the state support that was rebuilding mosques along with Orthodox churches. We visited one of these state-supported mosques, and it was indeed an elegant and well-crafted structure, overflowing with a crowd that seemed to be largely from the Caucasus region. Olga Leonova, a professor of sociology at Lomonosov, explained that Russian society has no problem with "ordinary Muslims," but some of the ones from the Caucasus region were influenced by separatist ideologies that were common in Chechnya, as well as a radical *jihadi* ideology that was sometimes associated with it. The Muslim representative explained, however, that the main issue with Chechnya was political, not religious. From a religious point of view, he insisted, Muslims were treated fairly, and no limitations were put on their religious activities.

The discussion shifted to other matters, but this brief exchange illustrated two profoundly similar tendencies regarding the social role of religion in the global age. It was soothing, in that it provided familiar practices and identities that reminded Russians of their deep heritage and the profound bonds of spirituality that united most of them and that touched on a legacy that reached back through centuries. At the same time, it was often resistant to change, especially regarding the acceptance of an emerging multicultural society. As we found out in Russia, Orthodox leaders were not the only ones asserting their influence in the public arena. Non-Orthodox Christians and

Muslims, especially newcomers from the Caucasus region and Kazakhstan, were trying to stake their own claims to Russian identity and social acceptance. The leadership of the Orthodox Church said that they welcomed these new groups, and perhaps they did. Still, from the perspective of many of the minorities and the newcomers, it is the church that is the most resistant to change. In the previous chapter, we saw how religious institutions and leaders have been buffeted by the storms of globalization and the currents of antiauthoritarian popularism that characterize the global age. In this chapter, we look at several responses—resistance, on the one hand, and creatively embracing the multicultural global era, on the other.

HOW RELIGION RESISTS

The Russian clergy are not the only religious conservatives who are defensive about traditional religion and wary of social change. Their counterparts in the United States and Western Europe, the Christian religious right, are at least as vocal about nationalism, on the one hand, and their fear of multiculturalism, on the other. At times, these passions have led to violence. Many conservative American Christians imagine that Muslims in their country are a threat to the American way of life. According to the television evangelist Pat Robertson, Islam is "not a religion," but a political ideology that is "demonic" and "bent on world domination."[1] Alas, he is not alone in this way of thinking, that has led to violent assaults on Muslims living in the United States, Europe, and elsewhere. When Anders Brevik attacked a youth camp in Norway in 2011, killing seventy-seven young people who were supporters of a liberal political party, his real target was the multiculturalism of a modern European society that he thought would bring about the destruction of traditional culture.

Resistance is a common response of many religious activists to a global era that challenges traditional ideas of identity, authority, and security. While some see the plurality that comes with international migration as promising deeper understanding among people, others feel their identity and ways of understanding the world challenged by an influx of outsiders. Religious institutions and their leaders often regard such changes as a danger to their way of life and to a social order that they regard as divinely blessed. That is where religion and xenophobia can become intertwined. All notions of nationhood are imagined, as the anthropologist Benedict Anderson has observed, and these imagined communities have imagined pasts that give foundation to the identities that unite them.[2] Religious leaders' attempts to create or re-create such a past bolsters the common core of their community and cements their own authority.

The idea of an "imagined past" does not suggest that historical events did not happen or that their importance was inflated. It recognizes, however, that history is often rewritten and usually abridged to favor society's winners. Alternative beliefs about what happened in the past—what others think *really* happened—have a great deal to do with changing social structures. Any conception of history is filtered in transmission; certain aspects of the past are brought to the fore and others are hidden, which results in an idealized version of history. The past is not remembered; it is constructed. Religion provides a particularly effective framework for the re-creation, as the past is constructed in alignment with accepted narratives about the way the world should be.

Such a move is evident in some of the religious responses to globalization in the Middle East, according to Mohammed Bamyeh, a professor of sociology at the University of Pittsburgh who comes from a Palestinian family. Bamyeh observed that "much of religious mobilization in the Middle East has become conservative" in a way that it had not been before, in part "to preserve the cultural integrity of society" in an era of global social changes.[3] That integrity is a result of common cultural practices and identities based around a sense of belonging. It seeks to impart what it means to be Tunisian or Lebanese, or even Arab or Muslim, by pointing to forms of being that are common to communities of the area.

This conservatism may, in part, stem from the fear of what Ayatollah Khomeini once described as "Westoxification," an inebriation of things Western. At the time of the Iranian Revolution in 1979, the new government led by the ayatollah was as concerned about the erosion of cultural values in the period of Western influence permitted by the shah as it was with the West's economic and political power over the country. In other areas of Asia, Africa, and the Middle East, the spread of symbols of Western economic influence—including the ubiquitous Coca-Cola vending machines and McDonald's hamburger franchises—have symbolized a new economic and cultural colonialism sponsored by the West in general and America in particular. In order to combat such a threat, some religious institutions have promoted a return to forms of life that existed prior to European colonialism, which abated only in the last century. Bamyeh pointed to the Muslim

Brotherhood, so influential in the post-revolution politics of Egypt's Arab Spring protests, as one of the main groups to deploy such a move. The implication is that their form of religious politics can resist the tide of Westernization and globalization and return the country to an imagined simpler past.

Many of these new right-wing religious movements around the world aim not just at political change but also at social change, and they embrace traditional cultural values. For this reason, many new religious movements are opposed not only to Western influence on politics but also to foreign efforts to provide health services, economic relief, and social support. Samah Faried, a former political advisor for the European Union in Cairo, noted during our Cairo workshop that many in Egypt—especially the powerful right-wing Islamic groups—were hostile to the influence of international nongovernmental humanitarian organizations.[4] Considering that such international humanitarian movements act in what they believe is the best interest of others, why should they be so feared?

One of the participants in our Cairo workshop, Amr Abdulrahman, political organizer for the Egyptian National Congress, argued that the answer lies in fear, primarily the fear of outside influence on Egyptian affairs. This fear has roots deep in Egyptian history. Abdulrahman explained how the opposition to foreign funding was part of the revolutionary program of 1952 that ultimately overthrew the Egyptian monarchy.[5] Led by the Free Officers Movement, Egyptian military officials wrested power from King Farouk and his British backers, ending what amounted to foreign rule over Egypt. As the revolution began to transform into an expressly Egyptian government, the focus on foreign influence was at the forefront of concerns. That led to an explosion of Egyptian nationalism, the rise of the Muslim Brotherhood as a national player, and an emphasis on domestic affairs. Nearly sixty years later, this spirit of resistance continues to be a factor in the attitude to foreign influence—from both official state policy and private aid workers.

Southeast Asia also has seen an increase in right-wing religious nationalism in recent decades, according to Siti Syamsiyatun, a participant in our Shanghai workshop and director of the Indonesian Consortium for Religious Studies. Again, fear seems to motivate the religious resistance to change. She said that although Islam in Indonesia has traditionally been moderate and tolerant of religious diversity, in recent years there has been a rise in the more rigid, conservative forms of Islam associated with the Salafi religiosity that is prominent in Saudi Arabia. Syamsiyatun noted that the promotion of polygamy and large families is foremost among new ideas infiltrating Indonesia, compelling some feminist groups to find ways to protect their community against the outside Salafi influence, while still maintaining their connection to the religion.[6]

As an activist for women's issues in Indonesia, Syamsiyatun noted that the struggle for women's rights in Indonesia has to be framed in Muslim terms in order to be widely accepted. She noted that there has been a surge in Muslim women scholars since the 1990s, and now they are challenging the traditional leadership to be accepted as equals. Traditionally, she said, males who have a high school education are entitled to the title of scholar, *Ulema*, but women require a doctorate for the same status. Opposition to this discrimination is growing. But the Muslim feminist movement in Indonesia has been careful to base their positions on traditional Islamic principle. Couching opposition to polygamy, for instance, in terms of gender equality rather than religious doctrine would result in resistance from male scholars opposed to what they might regard as "Western ideas."[7] So they point to the rights of women that were advocated by the Prophet himself and that have been a part of Muslim tradition.

Even organizations such as Indonesia's Muhammadiyah movement, which was founded upon a blend of Western and Islamic ideas and is known for engaging in myriad social programs in Indonesia, are beginning to shore up their Muslim identities rather than participating in more interfaith projects. An article by A. N. Burhani, an Indonesian scholar who was in our workshops, examined the relationship between Muhammadiyah and other civil society groups to show that two Islamic precepts illustrate the way the organization has engaged with other groups in recent years.[8] The first is that of *fa-istabiqū al-khayrāt*,[9] which means "to compete with one another in good works" and has long been considered by scholars to form the core of Islamic interfaith pluralism. Burhani asserts, however, that many in the Muhammadiyah movement are now interpreting this precept as a guide to relations only with other Islamic organizations, while interaction with non-Muslims are meant to follow another principle, the idea of *lakum dīnukum wa-liya dīnī*,[10] meaning "unto you your religion, and unto me my religion." This principle is interpreted as seeing other religious groups as rivals rather than competitors, with the former carrying a more negative connotation than the latter and creating an environment of conflict instead of possible cooperation.

This defensive interpretation is not the only one, nor is it fixed in stone, according to workshop participant Mark Woodward. He noted that when people needed to work together on a common cause, they would often say, "you may be a Baptist and you may be a Catholic, and I may be NU [a member of Nahdlatul Ulama, another Islamic group in Indonesia], and she may be from Muhammadiyah, but for these purposes, we're going to put those differences aside."[11] The key, according to Woodward, is the social context, and whether isolationism or interaction appears more advantageous to the issues at hand. Other participants in our workshops pointed to the importance of making a distinction between politics and culture. Muhamad Ali, a professor of religious studies at the University of California, Riverside, who was born in Jakarta, noted that engaging in politics marks a group as being dangerous, while operating on a more cultural level is seen as innocuous. "In the field of culture," Ali said, "it is easy for Muhammadiyah to cooperate with other religious organizations, Muslim and non-Muslim."[12]

At the same time, it is possible for Muslim groups in Indonesia to be devoted to social service and still be narrowly sectarian. This was the point made by another workshop participant, Mary Zurbuchen, who lived in the country for many years and was formerly the Ford Foundation's director of Asia and Russia programs. She discussed how some Muslim groups in Indonesia engage in social-service projects while explicitly promoting an antipluralist agenda. It was not that they were unaware of other faiths and other varieties of Islam—quite the opposite. Interfaith contacts have been accelerated by the processes of globalization, but they have evoked fears about group solidarity. Some groups have exploited such fears to increase their recruitment. According to Zurbuchen, "the issue of *murtad*, of apostasy" is raised by the challenges of Christian evangelists, and Muslims from a Salafi perspective have promoted the idea that "prolonged exposure to Christians could be dangerous." The prestige of some of the Muslim extremists who make these claims is enhanced by their pretensions to authority in the matter.[13]

In other parts of the world, the emphasis on intense, personal forms of religiosity can encourage the believers to become more socially active and more tolerant to others. An example of this is the phenomenon of Christian "cell groups" in Central and South America. At our workshop on Latin America and the Caribbean, Virginia Garrard-Burnett, a professor of religious studies at the University of Texas, Austin, described these cell groups as consisting of small numbers of Christians who meet together regularly to study the Bible, sometimes up to four times a week. Rather than considering the theological implications of the scriptures, their focus is centered on what lessons the Bible can offer about life in the world. "They apply the Bible to their lives," Garrard-Burnett said, raising questions such as, " 'if I'm a changed person, how does that play out in society?'" and " 'how do you cope in a world where you don't drink alcohol anymore?'"[14] The religious text serves as a way for them to enter into larger questions about the role of the person in society.

Yet these cell groups, which Garrard-Burnett notes are "widespread in Latin American Protestant groups and charismatic groups,"[15] have consequences on civil society in general. Their focus on how redemption can change the world can be applied to larger assemblages, and a focus on the local can be channeled into effects on an international level. For instance, Garrard-Burnett notes that some politicians, such as Harold Caballeros, the leader of a major political party in Guatemala, "have actively pushed for the increase of the cellular groups and want to expand this idea of redemption to the whole country."[16] These groups do not vote as a bloc, nor do they mobilize their members as a unit, but they can still wield substantial influence on society.

Meanwhile, in Latin America, the traditional Roman Catholic Church hierarchy is largely perceived as defending the status quo. In our Buenos Aires workshop, this observation was underscored by Kurt Frieder, director of *Fundacion Huesped,* the largest organization in South America dedicated to improving the lives of people living with HIV/AIDS. He was dismayed at the church's unwillingness to engage with changes in the world. According to Frieder, in Argentina and throughout Latin America, "local conservative groups still hold great power" and in those circles "the Catholic Church's voice and opinion is almost decisive when it comes to some conflictive matters related to education, health, and civil-society activity."[17]

There are also instances of religious leaders consciously trying to extricate religion from the messy business of politics. In Iran, one of the most religious regimes on earth, Muslim theologians have pleaded with the ruling clergy to free Islam from politics. Abdolkarim Soroush, acclaimed as Iran's most influential scholar, has argued that Islam should be practiced separately from political affairs for the sake of both religion and politics. The legal scholar Abdullahi Ahmed an-Na'im, who teaches at Emory University Law School, has written a compelling book presenting ideas first formulated by the great Sudanese theologian Mahmoud Mohammed Taha, arguing that shari'ah law should not be imposed on believers but voluntarily embraced; hence, the best form of political order for a Muslim country is secular.[18] When we were in Cairo and met with the Grand Mufti of Egypt, as we noted earlier, he too insisted that Islam should be free from politics, implying that the Muslim Brotherhood was employing religion largely for political purposes.

In Kenya, there has been a turn away from religious politics. At one time, Christian churches and Islamic institutions in the country played a political role in encouraging the country to turn toward more open and democratic political systems, but in more recent years, religious leaders of both faiths have become less involved.[19]

The efforts of the Christians and Muslims in Kenya to escape politics are a way of distancing religion from state power and the status quo. But they are also a way of disengaging from the world. In its own way, it is also a form of resistance to the winds of global change that are sweeping through the world. For the individual believer, a retreat to personal piety may come as a relief, since perhaps more than anything else, religious beliefs and private practices can offer a balm of comfort in a bruised and battered world.

HOW RELIGION SOOTHES

Though religion often resists global change, it also provides soothing alternatives. Personal piety is one way that religion provides a salve of comfort at times of social turmoil. Another is identity—the sense of belonging to a stable and comforting community.

Take the situation of Nigeria, for example. In the northern part of the country extremist militants such as Boko Haram have ravished the countryside, slaughtered villagers, and kidnapped young schoolgirls from their classrooms. In other parts of the country, corruption and ethnic tensions wreak havoc on public life. There are two main religious affiliations in the country—Islam in the north and Christianity in the south. Though they can be utilized for extremism and violence, for most Nigerians these communities of faith are ports of safety in stormy social seas.

Nigerian scholar Jacob Olupona, professor of African and African American religion at Harvard, spoke about the growing social importance of religion in Africa at our workshop on Africa and the Middle East. Olupona said that when divisions of ethnicity become too contentious in a country like Nigeria, political leaders "often turn to conservative forms of religion to build their constituency."[20] Religious bonds are able to provide a secure identity that transcends narrow tribal allegiances but do not rely on the political agenda of nationalism or any other ideology perceived as foreign.

The construction of a religious identity—like any other group identity—relies on an external point of reference, a "them" that we can point to and define as "not us." Religion constructs these boundaries in a number of ways, basing them in belief, social or linguistic components, or geographic locale. Whichever aspect of personhood is highlighted, it always has a counterpart in the wider world: those who believe or practice or look different. Such a process marks those outside the group as "other." In times of peace, it is comforting for people to know who "we" are and that "we" are not "them." In times of crisis, the other can become demonized, can be made the cause of one's woes. Either way, religious identity provides a feeling of solidarity; one can trust those in one's community.

In the twentieth century, this sense of social solidarity was created by nationalism. It was enough to consider oneself Nigerian or American, German or Indonesian. These nationalist identities carried an implicit recognition that the needs and causes of one's fellow countrymen and countrywomen would be placed above those of other countries. In the global era, however, nationalism—along with the political autonomy of the nation-state—is under siege. The changing global infrastructure is radically challenging those sources of identity. Large groups of Turks now live in Germany; Mexicans and Asians are flooding into the United States. Boundaries that had previously determined belonging have become porous, and populations are interwoven to such a degree that the problems of one country can put a great deal of strain on others. People who decide to live outside the country of their birth are no longer cut off from the families and communities they left behind, and that continued relationship has taken the emphasis off assimilation into the new culture.

At the same time that these global demographic shifts are changing the ethnic character of traditional societies, the weakening of the nation-state in an era of globalization has unleashed internal tensions that were previously stifled, usually through autocratic rule. Hence, in such places as Nigeria and Indonesia, as well as in Iraq and Syria, ethnic tensions have flourished. In the latter cases, religion has compounded the problem by being linked with particular ethnic groups. In other cases, such as Indonesia, religion provides an alternative identity that unifies a people beyond nationalist borders. And in yet other cases, religion is fused with a revived nationalism, as it has been in Iran and Russia and among right-wing Christian nationalists in Europe and the United States.

In places where immigrant populations are upsetting the traditional communities, religion often provides a secure social location. In the United States, for example, large numbers of Korean immigrants convert to Christianity and are able to fit into America's dominantly Christian culture through their own form of ethnic Christianity. In Europe, immigrants from Algeria, Turkey, Pakistan, and other Muslim countries come together to worship in mosques that are often accepted into European society as alternative forms of religiosity within a common nationalist umbrella. In Oslo, for example, the Norwegian government has authorized the construction of a handsome modern mosque prominently located in the downtown area, demonstrating the nation's attempt to accept the reality of its new multicultural identities.

Rather than trying to assimilate completely into the new national culture, immigrants often try to do both—relate to their new surroundings and maintain their family traditions, thanks to improved communications and movement technologies. Benedict Anderson has called these "email/internet nationalisms."[21] The result is not a melting pot, in which all are spiced by each other's culture, but more of a cultural stew: an increased multiculturalism where numerous cultures exist side by side. Although globalization has often been accused of being a force of homogenization, intent on making all cultures look like Western Europeans, its dynamics has also led to an increased cultural heterogeneity within Europe and the United States as well.

This new multiculturalism works well in many areas. But it is also resisted, both by some members of the immigrant community, who, like angry young Algerians in Paris, feel that they are neither one thing nor another, not really Algerian or French. And it is also resisted by conservative elements in the host country that fear social change. It is this attitude that propelled people such as televangelist Pat Robertson in the United States to rail against Muslims and motivated Anders Brevik in Norway to attack a youth camp for a political party that supported multiculturalism. In Myanmar (formerly Burma), the angry religious nationalists are Buddhists: Ashin Wirathu, a Buddhist monk, has imagined hordes of Muslims swarming into his country from Bangladesh and demolishing Myanmar's traditional culture.

Such people see multiculturalism as a threat to their way of life and identity. The us-versus-them way of thinking has defined citizenship for so long that a conception of identity beyond that seems inconceivable. This constructed dichotomy has long been seen as inevitable, but it need not remain that way. In the words of one of our workshop participants, Surichai Wun'gaeo, "we are trapped by national identities, but human identity could go beyond."[22] The onset of globalization, therefore, can provide an opportunity to escape the in-group/out-group mentality that has defined communities for most of human history by replacing it with a transnational identity, with a focus on common values supported by a variety of religious communities.

In the meantime, religious identities formed around the world's great faith communities provide a host of social benefits. They can also play a significant role in soothing the transition to a more globalized world. As we have just seen in the case of the Muslim mosque in Oslo, religion can provide a basis of identity that is not necessarily threatening to national identities and can reside within a multicultural framework under the aegis of the nation-state. Faith communities also provide networks of support. This was the point made by James Wellman, a sociologist at the University of Washington's Jackson School of International Studies at our workshop on Latin America and the Caribbean, when he said that such communities "give culture a network and allow people to survive because they care for one another and build up social capital" that gives them social support in the wider society.[23] According to Wellman, these communities provide "a durable network of more-or-less institutionalized relationships of mutual acquaintance and recognition."[24]

Such networks are no longer confined to geographic realities. At our Shanghai workshop, Tadaatsu Tajima of Japan's Tenshi College noted the importance of faith connections that span geographic locations. According to Tajima, "the Catholic Church, as well as many other religions, retains an ability to provide a nest for 'birds of immigrant feathers to flock together,'" adding that "religion provides old and new immigrants a place to recognize their own identity; therefore, they can survive in the host country, feeling safe at home."[25] As global religious institutions are unbound by nationality, they can provide a haven in any country. The newly arrived faithful find instant networks of support, making housing, employment, and companionship easier to find.

For those uprooted from their native community and attempting to find their place in a new country, a religious identity can smooth a difficult transition. One of our Shanghai workshop participants, Master Kai Sheng, a professor of philosophy at Tsinghua University of China and a Buddhist monk, shared how people at times take on a religious identity even when it is not normally how they understand themselves. "Ordinary Chinese people do not believe that Buddhism is an identity," Sheng said, but then he described Chinese people he knew who went abroad to do business. "Back home, they don't have a religious identity," he said, "but when they go abroad . . . they will use Buddhism as a religious identity."[26]

Moreover, the forces of globalization are having an impact beyond just business travelers, according to Sheng. Where there is a multitude of possible identities, there is anxiety and disorientation, and "more choices mean no choice." In such situations, Sheng continued, people need a religious identity in order to find their location in a sea of globalization.[27]

THE REINVENTION OF RELIGION

As we have seen in this chapter, traditional faith communities around the world have responded to the turmoil of global changes by resisting, on the one hand, and providing soothing networks of support, on the other. But—to strain the metaphor—there are other hands, other ways of responding to globalization, and religious communities have been adapting in creative ways.

Throughout history, religious traditions have survived, in large part, because of their ability to adapt to the cultural contexts in which they are rooted. Though believers will claim that the heart of their religion has not changed, and perhaps this is true, the way that believers interact with others often has. In the current multicultural environment, one of these changes is a focus on values that can be shared across sectarian lines—through interfaith alliances—in addition to identities and beliefs that are, by their natures, specific and culturally divisive.

At the Shanghai workshop, Somboon Chungprampree, a Thai Buddhist who is a representative of the International Network of Engaged Buddhists, spoke about the harmonizing role that religion can play in an increasingly connected world. He focused on three concepts that most religious traditions share: justice, reverence for nature, and spiritual development.[28]

According to Chungprampree, these three values can be appreciated by members of any faith. Changing the focus from the politics of identity to a sense of shared spiritual depth can foster interfaith cooperation across borders.

The possibilities of interfaith collaboration were a popular theme in our workshops. In Delhi, Ranjana Mukhopadhyaya, a faculty member in the department of East Asian studies at Delhi University, talked about how Muslim and Buddhist communities worked together after a flood tore through the region of Ladakh. Ladakh is in the state of Jammu and Kashmir, which is claimed by both India and Pakistan and has seen recurring violence over the dispute. Religious politics come into play, since most of the people in Kashmir are Muslim, and Pakistan was carved out of the Indian subcontinent at the time of independence in 1948 to provide a secular locus for people with Muslim identities. What complicates the Kashmir situation is the large Hindu population still living there, and the fact that the rule of the state of Kashmir prior to independence was Indian-administered and preferred the region to continue to be ruled by India. The area of Ladakh complicates the picture even more, since most of its citizens are neither Muslim nor Hindu, but Buddhist. Some even call it "Little Tibet," though it also contains a sizable Muslim community. The fact that Muslims and Buddhists could work together in that area in a time of intense flooding is a testimony to the ability of people to reach across faith boundaries and cooperate on issues of common concern.

This cooperation did not occur in a vacuum. Mukhopadhyaya and her colleagues had been trying to encourage interfaith relations in Ladakh for some time. They had convened members of the Buddhist and Muslim communities in Ladakh for a dialogue, and only a month after the groups met, a cloudburst sent torrents of rain into the arid, mountainous region causing floods and mudslides. Many Ladakh villagers were caught completely unprepared for such a natural disaster. In part because the groundwork for cooperation had so recently been laid between Muslim and Buddhist leaders, a great deal of assistance was quickly secured from outside agencies in a collaborative way.[29]

Another example of how interfaith cooperation has brought international attention was offered by Rosalind Hackett of the University of Tennessee, an expert on religion in Africa who participated in our Africa and the Middle East workshop. When she was in Uganda in 2004, she found that the Lord's Resistance Army, which would gain infamy in later years, was engaged in a conflict with the government of Uganda's President Museveni. Hackett was "struck by the neglect—the national and international neglect—and lack of interest in what was an extreme humanitarian and political crisis."[30] What brought this crisis to international attention was the Acholi Religious Leaders Peace Initiative (ARLPI), an interreligious organization of Anglican, Catholic, and Muslim communities in Uganda.

A similar story about an interfaith group giving voice to the voiceless came from our workshop on South and Southeast Asia. There, Surichai Wun'gaeo spoke about the Coordinating Group for Religion and Society (CGRS), a small group of Catholics, Protestants, Buddhists, and Muslims working for civil rights in 1970s Thailand. The CGRS used their global networks to bring awareness to the issue of violent repression during a coup that ousted the government.[31]

Another way that religion reinvents itself through being open to the shared values of other religious traditions is by affirming a common spiritual depth at the heart of all religious communities. This is the spiritual side of interfaith relations. In California, for instance, local Episcopal churches hold yoga classes without any sense that this Hindu practice is inappropriate for a Christian church. It is a spiritual practice, after all, and spirituality is spirituality. T. N. Madan, perhaps India's most distinguished sociologist, suggested during our workshop in New Delhi that it was precisely outside of the formal institutions of Hinduism that "the riches of the South Asian perspective may be discovered."[32] These, Madan implied, could be appreciated by people of all faiths.

The logical extension of this way of thinking is to see the spirituality of all aspects of life, even in ideologies and movements that are not explicitly religious. When polls are taken about religious identity in the United States, the group that is growing the fastest is not Christian or Muslim or atheist, but those who choose "none of the above." These "nones," as we mentioned earlier in this book, often describe themselves as "spiritual, not religious." They are not opposed to religious ideas and practices, but they are not affiliated with any particular organization or tradition. As we saw in our last chapter, increasingly, the organized forms of religion are learning to live with the "nones."

An example of the way that this anti-institutional attitude toward religion has affected traditional religion is found in the Philippines. In our workshop in Shanghai, Dominador Bombongan, dean of the College of Liberal Arts at De La Salle University of the Philippines, gave the example of Catholic and Episcopal Filipino youth. While young people in the Philippines have become less and less concerned with regular attendance at church and participation in other traditional church activities, they still consider themselves Christian. Their focus has shifted from the doctrinal dimension of the church to a more experiential dimension; they desire practical guidance in their day-to-day lives rather than abstract concepts. Religion has become more personal for these youths, "something that inspires [them] to goodness," Bombongan said, "rather than frightening [them] with hellfire."[33]

In Muslim countries, too, there are signs of openness to less rigid forms of religiosity in the era following the Arab Spring in 2011, which resulted in a shift in political and religious perspective across a great many countries. According to Mohammed Bamyeh, the religion found in countries such as Tunisia and Egypt and Morocco after the Arab Spring was "not the same religion that you see in the prerevolutionary period." He went on to explain that it was impossible to imagine "that everyone will just stay with their old ideas forever and not be influenced by the transformations that are happening."[34]

It would be a simple conclusion to say that these young people in the Philippines and Egypt are becoming secularized. Rather, Bombongan sees these young people as illustrative of a process of reflexivity brought on by the current age. The increased perspective offered by global processes is not destroying local expressions through a cultural homogenization but rather is allowing people to see that there is not just one way to be a Catholic, a Christian, a Buddhist, or a Muslim. So many variations exist on a religious theme that people can determine *how* they want to be religious. Such a situation requires solutions based in the local contexts that people exist within. As Jeffrey Haynes remarked, in discussing the changes in the global, it is important to stay oriented to the local.[35]

Part of the reason why religion is able to reinvent itself—adapt to different cultural contexts—is that it is always at least in part a local phenomenon. The authority of the papacy gives the illusion that the Roman Catholic Church is a uniform institution, and the centrality of Mecca gives the appearance that all Muslims think and act the same. But in both cases, the realities on the ground are much more complicated. "There is no such thing as Catholicism," said Jennifer Hughes, a professor at the University of California at Riverside, at our workshop on Latin America and the Caribbean. By that, she meant that there is no monolithic thing that one can call "Catholicism" in the singular. Rather, Hughes said, we need to focus on specific communities in their individual context. Hughes thought we need a local view, "a local approach to looking at global Christianities."[36] Virginia Garrard-Burnett echoed that point later at that workshop. She talked about the Pentecostal communities in Guatemala, describing them as "hydra-headed" to affirm that theirs is not a single movement, but a diverse body of networks and agendas.[37]

Because they are local, religious communities in their diversity can more easily adapt to the cultural environments around them. They might become defensive and escapist, as we have seen earlier in this chapter, but they are poised to be able to respond creatively to the cultural contexts in which they reside. As Hughes says, these local groups can "preserve, shape, and narrate very specific community identities."[38] Hence, local religious communities can preserve old cultural forms or be open to new ones.

And they can do both at once. Robert Dowd, director of the Ford Program at Notre Dame's Kellogg Institute for International Studies in our Africa and Middle East workshop, made this point when discussing the women of Côte d'Ivoire, stressing that they "would see themselves as truly Christian . . . and as truly traditional at the same time."[39] It is not a matter of having to choose between mutually exclusive identities presented as an either/or, "religious" or wholly "traditional." These women can see themselves as both Christian and modern, or Christian and global citizens. As Dowd observed, we can be many things to many people, all at the same time. "The world is very complicated," Dowd noted, adding, "religious identities are very complex and nuanced."[40] Those complex identities can allow for greater flexibility when dealing with the challenges of the global age, and at times, they can help bring people into a greater awareness of the problems facing people elsewhere in the world.

As we have seen in this chapter, these complex identities can create division among people of the same locale, separating them into the in-groups and the out-groups. At the same time, the shifting context of global changes can lead to new forms of religious creativity and openness. As Elizabeth Collins, professor of world religions and Southeast Asian studies at the University of Ohio, put it at our South and Southeast Asia workshop, figures such as Mohandas Gandhi, the Dalai Lama, and Mahmoud Muhammad Taha have shown that the religious impulse can "make us rise to our better selves."[41] In the twenty-first century, this humanistic characteristic of religion can pave the way to a universal expression of global spirituality. It is to this possibility that we turn in the next chapter.

"Christopher Columbus in the Americas," Buenos Aires. Photograph by Dinah Griego.

FOUR

Cosmopolitan Religion at Work

HOW RELIGIOUS VALUES SUPPORT
GLOBAL CITIZENSHIP

BUENOS AIRES, THE STAR OF Argentina, is one of the most European cities we've visited, and yes, we've spent a good bit of time in London, Paris, Berlin, Madrid, and the rest. What is European about Buenos Aires is not just the architecture—though the broad streets lined with early twentieth-century magisterial stone structures do evoke images of the grand monuments of Imperial Britain—but also the people. They tend to be white, the term we often use to designate people of European ancestry, but of various shades. There are Brits and Spaniards and Germans and Italians—lots of Italians. At one time, Buenos Aires was such an Italian-dominant community that the residents wanted Argentina to drop Spanish as the country's official language and adopt Italian instead. The rest of the country resisted, and Argentina remains a Spanish-speaking nation, despite the ethnic diversity of its people.

With all these Spaniards and Italians, one would expect the Roman Catholic Church to flourish, and this is indeed the case. But there is also a sizable Jewish community, a portion of which came as refugees from Nazi tyranny. At the same time, some former Nazi sympathizers fled Germany to Argentina after World War II, and there they are in Buenos Aires, side by side with German Jews. Increasingly, there are members of other religious traditions as well—Muslims, Hindus, Buddhists, and Sikhs—but the country and its main city are dominantly Catholic.

The residents of Buenos Aires are Catholic, however, in a kind of European way. A certain loyalty to the church is maintained on holidays and respected as long as it doesn't interfere too much with their personal lives, especially in matters of sexuality and family planning. Over the church's boisterous objections, the country's legislators have refused to prohibit abortions, and in 2010

Argentina became the first Latin American country to legalize same-sex marriage. Both measures are overwhelming popular with the Argentine public, especially in worldly Buenos Aires. As we noted earlier, in the years before he received the papal crown in 2013, when Pope Francis was Archbishop Jorge Bergoglio in Buenos Aires, he vocally challenged these measures, but he was drowned out by the voices of secularism and tolerant liberalism. But perhaps the word *secularism* is too strong to describe people who, as we say, are nominally Catholic but independent minded and open to diversity.

So when we held our workshop on religion in global civil society in Buenos Aires, we convened an interesting, and quite representative, Argentine mix. There were several who strongly identified as Catholics or Jews and who were tied to the religious institutions of their communities. But there were also scholars and social activists who did not identify with religion at all and were often critical of the Catholic hierarchy, especially in matters relating to AIDS education and abortion rights. Yet with regard to everything else, there were remarkably few differences among them. Like many contemporary gatherings, it was not apparent what people's religious affiliations were, or whether they had any at all, even in fairly serious conversation. This was the case even when the discussions turned to matters of morality, cultural values, and the spiritual dimension of contemporary society. Secular or religious, the participants shared common assumptions about civic responsibility and the need for a moral community.

At the Buenos Aires workshop, when the discussion turned to income inequality and the plight of the poor in the country, the concern was profound, and it came from all sides. Whether their inspiration for social justice was grounded in the Gospels or the writings of Karl Marx, the result was the same: the participants regarded inequality as bad not just for those who suffered economic oppression as a result of it but also for the vitality of the public community as a whole. At issue was a sense that the present situation of globalization, with its corporate exploitation and media homogenization, was an assault on the moral and spiritual underpinnings of the public community. This was interesting. It was almost as if these citizens, whether Catholic, Jewish, or secular, shared a new, common religion that supported a culture of civic concern.

We don't quite know what to call this common religio-secular morality, though we see examples of it all around us, not just in Buenos Aires, but also in urban settings around the world. And the communities about which they are concerned are not just within their own nationalist boundaries; they are also concerned about their region and ultimately the world. An activist in our workshop who was promoting AIDS education traveled throughout South America to set up local groups of supporters, and though the network was based in Buenos Aires, all of its participants regarded themselves as part of a common family. In a global era, increasingly these moral communities span continents and oceans. The network of concern regarding environmental issues, for example, is truly worldwide.

This expanded moral consciousness constitutes one of the most interesting aspects of religion in the global era. It may be a sign of a new religiosity and morality that has emerged in the cosmopolitan cultures of the interconnected world. Though the traditional religions often support many of these common values, the expression of it seems to be distinctly something else, an emerging culture of a global civil society.

IS THERE A GLOBAL CIVIL SOCIETY?

To answer the question of whether there is such a thing as a global civil society, and whether it can spawn a culture that has moral and spiritual depth, we consulted with one of the great sociological minds of the contemporary era: Robert Bellah. Bellah, who taught at the University of California at Berkeley for most of his career, was an old friend of ours and graciously took up the challenge, coming down the California coast to Santa Barbara to join our discussions. At the time, Bellah had just completed his magisterial seven-hundred-page volume *Religion in Human Evolution,* and he was eager to talk about it.[1] To some extent, the issues that absorbed him in this book corresponded with some of the ideas in our project, since Bellah was trying to understand what was the common religious element that united all people (and all species, for that matter) on the planet, from the beginning of time to relatively recent civilizational development. Bellah was looking at global religious culture through historical epochs from early forms of conscious life to the Axial Age around the sixth century BCE, when thinkers such as Plato, Confucius, and the Buddha were nearly simultaneously expressing new forms of thinking about moral and spiritual ways of being. So the issue of whether there is a common religious culture today was not too much of a stretch for him.

Our interests were even more closely related, however, to an earlier Bellah essay. In 1967 he published "Civil Religion in America," in which he analyzed the inaugural speeches of U.S. presidents and determined that their invocation of religious metaphors and concepts was done not just to appeal to religious voters but also to chart out a kind of religion of Americanism, to state that American society was itself a moral and spiritual community.[2] The essay had an enormous impact on sociological thinking about America's political culture when it was first published, and it continues to do so. Bellah joked that some people think that it is the only thing that he has written.

The notion of civil religion did not come out of thin air, however; it had some solid intellectual foundations. The term that he used, *civil religion,* was first employed by the European Enlightenment thinker Jean-Jacques Rousseau in the eighteenth century to describe the moral and spiritual character of what we otherwise think of as "secular" political society.[3] But Bellah looked to the concepts of French sociologist Émile Durkheim before Rousseau. Durkheim regarded all collectivities of having a religious element, the glue that holds societies together around a common set of totemic symbols and shared values.[4] In the Durkheimian sense, it was natural that a country would have its own "religion," a shared set of values and symbols that gave it the emotional integrity to cohere. This is what Bellah called *civil religion* in America.

We wanted to know whether Bellah thought there could be a *global* civil religion. We wanted to know if he thought that the same elements of shared values and symbolic expressions of unity could be—and are in the process of being—fused into something that could be construed as a global culture, even a global religion. Characteristically, in thinking about these questions, Bellah shaped his answer in the form of a written paper and a formal presentation.

Part of the reason he was interested enough in the topic to write an essay on the question, we believe, stemmed from the fact that Bellah was already thinking ahead to his next book, the sequel to *Religion in Human Evolution,* which would deal with the evolution of religion in the last several millennia, especially with the emergence of individualism and rationality in the eighteenth-century European Enlightenment, concepts that are the bulwark of the rationalism and secularism of today. So for Bellah, this topic was an opportunity to think beyond the secular-religion dichotomy, as we described it in the introductory chapter of this book, and to think of the possibilities of a global religion.

His unpublished paper, "Is Global Civil Society Possible?" was presented at Santa Barbara on February 2, 2012.[5] It turned out to be one of his last essays, since Bellah died rather suddenly a little over a year later, on July 30, 2013, of complications related to heart surgery in a hospital near his home in Berkeley. He was eighty-six; he had had a long and varied career that made him one of the world's most discussed sociologists of religion.[6] Alas, his book on individualism, secularism, and the possibility of global civil religion will never be completed, but his Santa Barbara talk gives an insight into his thinking about these topics.

Bellah's Santa Barbara paper begins where his "Civil Religion in America" ends, with the possibility of what Bellah calls "a world civil religion." Bellah, quoting his own words in "Civil Religion in America," says that the time has come to consider global society as containing the elements of "a viable and coherent world order." Moreover, the cultural dimension of such a world order requires "a major new set of symbolic forms." This sounds like he is anticipating a global religion, though in the earlier essay he did not go into any detail about what these "symbolic forms" might be and how they would relate to traditional religion. His 2012 reflections in Santa Barbara began to elaborate on these two cryptic statements.

How could a global civil religion be constructed? As we interpret Bellah's essay, he argues that there are at least three possibilities. One would be a kind of synthesis of some of the moral and spiritual elements of all the religious traditions of humankind—such as Christianity, Islam, and the like—or if not a synthesis, at least a repository of their shared values. The second would be as an extension of the civil religions of America, Russia, and other national societies. The third would be an expression of an emerging new global culture.

While Bellah focuses on the third—the embryonic, cultural aspects of a new global society—he does talk about the possibility of traditional religion and nationalist civil religions participating in this emerging culture. One example of this latter possibility came to Bellah when he was in China in December 2010. He was surprised to discover how interested Chinese scholars were in the idea of a civil religion—not just for America, but also for China. These scholars could see the Confucian stratum of morality and shared spiritual values becoming a basis for a civil religion for Chinese society. But beyond that, Bellah reports, they were interested in a Chinese civil religion that would be "open to the rest of the world and perhaps participate in a global civil religion."

All of this sounds optimistic, but Bellah was not, by nature, an optimist. For one thing, he saw the difficulties in getting parochially minded people to look beyond their local and national interests to the profound economic, environmental, and social problems that confront humanity on this planet and that might unite them morally into a global civil society. For another, he saw the possibility that the notion of common global identity and purpose could be formed around functional and utilitarian economic interests rather than moral and social concerns.

This was the dismal observation made by the Harvard theologian Harvey Cox in an interesting paper included in a Festschrift for Bellah published in 2002. Cox wonders whether there is not already a global religion in the form of worshipping economic greed. In this essay, "Mammon and the Culture of the Market," Cox suggests that for many people around the world, the economic market is seen as more than a human creation; it is a "power beyond human control" that is "omnipotent, omniscient, and omnipresent."[7] Bellah speculates that Cox may be right, that the worship of this deity of the global market is something of a global religion. But it is not based on global civil society—quite the opposite, it fosters divisive ideologies and grave economic inequalities that undermine a sense of common purpose and collective concern.

So Cox's idea of a "market religion" is not, from Bellah's point of view, a true global religion. Bellah looks instead at another kind of enduring religiosity, the shared elements of interacting religious traditions over the centuries. Bellah regards this common history of the varied religions in the world to comprise one history, and in that sense, it is a global religion, though ultimately this kind of global religiosity is also insufficient without a sense of global civil society.

But it is significant, this sharing of religious culture over the centuries. Planetary trade and other forms of commerce have existed since the days of early explorers from Europe and China, and as people interacted, so have their cultures. Buddhism swept up from South Asia and spread throughout the Asian continent. Christianity took elements from Middle Eastern religion and transformed European culture. As these religious cultures spread, they absorbed local cultural elements and interacted with other traditions. Hence Christians observe the day of Jesus's birth with the evergreen tree revered by pagan Europeans during winter solstice, and the day of his resurrection, with the fertility symbols of the rabbit and eggs that were part of pre-Christian European festivals of the spring equinox.

As the Harvard historian of religion Wilfred Cantwell Smith has demonstrated, there has been a remarkable interaction of religious traditions over history. The story that Smith was fond of telling was the one about the Catholic rosary—the string of beads that is used by the faithful to count prayers. Smith traced the history of this practice and deduced that the Catholics got the idea from Muslims, among whom prayer beads are also a common artifact.[8] But Muslims most likely received the idea from Buddhists, who use prayer beads as well; and the Buddhists, in turn, learned about them from Indian Brahmans, whose 108 beads count the requisite number of Hindu prayers. If prayer beads can travel from religion to religion, from culture to culture, surely ideas can also—and likely have done so.

For these reasons, Bellah argues, the history of religion has been a single story. His *Religion in Human Evolution* charts the development of religiosity across the centuries as a single evolving planetary phenomenon, albeit one that is expressed in particular cultural identities, such as Hindu, Jewish, and Chinese.[9] But the singularity of the world's religious culture is not the same thing as global civil religion, Bellah argues, since this new kind of global religion is the expression of the new phenomenon of global civil society, the idea of a shared sense of citizenship. This is a recent notion, and the possibilities of a global religion in this sense, as an expression of global civil society, is just now emerging.

Thus the two ideas, global civil society and global religion, are linked. The latter is the cultural expression of the former. In his paper, Bellah traces the development of the idea of civil society from its inception in eighteenth-century Europe, when it was a part of the complex of ideas related to the European Enlightenment. "Civil society," in the Enlightenment context, described what Bellah calls "the public sphere, a realm of thought, argument, and association independent of the state, but leading to the formation of what came to be called public opinion." It is this notion of citizenship that is explored by Jürgen Habermas in *The Structural Transformation of the Public Sphere*.[10] The concepts of freedom of speech and freedom of religious expression are essential to the sense of citizenship in the public sphere, and they were enshrined in all of the leading Enlightenment documents, including those of the American Declaration of Independence and Constitution. The idea of universal human rights also became a part of the shared values of the civil society of the public sphere.

Civil society was initially thought to be something that was the province only of national societies. Increasingly in recent years, however, the notion of civil society has gone global, and the phrase *global civil society* has gained acceptance by scholars and social activists around the world. One of the reasons for this is the presumed universality of human rights. Another has been the pervasive growth of international NGOs, especially in the last twenty years. Yet another has been the rise of transnational social movements around such issues as economic equality, women's rights, and environmental protection. At the same time, the advent of instantaneous mass communication through cell phones and the internet has brought individuals together in an unparalleled way. In the twenty-first century, there is a global economy, global legal norms, global communications, and even global festivals such as the Olympics and the World Cup.

All of these developments have led toward networks of interaction not just among national elites but also among ordinary citizens—a global civil society. Increasingly, nation-state borders do not restrict whom or what we may contact, nor do they define our sense of community. At the same time, however, economic interaction on an international scale is creating another kind of global community, one that is very much focused on the transnational elites who control and profit from these flows of capital. This elite form of global economic activity is conducive neither to global civil society nor global religion, from Bellah's point of view. The question is whether the decentralized form of global citizenry can grow despite the attempts of a global elite to control it.

This is where Habermas's speculation about transnational governance comes into play. The emergence of a global civil society is a challenge to nationalist power and to global elite power, and it requires its own forms of power creation in response. Mass movements and international NGOs provide one kind of counterweight. Global public opinion, as voiced over the internet, is by far the most democratic of new communications media. Other challenges to national and elite power come from newly developed transnational agencies in dealing with problems of the environment, global communications, and the worldwide diasporas of peoples and cultures. Some of these agencies are supported by the United Nations; others have formed on their own, with support from interstate or transnational social movements. Habermas is buoyed by these developments and by regional entities such as the European Union, which he regards as the first step to moving beyond narrow nationalism.

Bellah, however, is less sanguine about the efficacy of these developments in creating a sense of global citizenship on their own, and he returns to the idea of building a moral consensus that can provide the basis for transnational institutions of accountability. Though he appreciates Habermas's attempts to think about a sense of citizenship beyond narrow nationalism, Bellah thinks that Habermas's notion of an "abstract constitutional patriotism" is an insufficient base for creating a global civil society. For that you need moral commitment. And this is where religion comes in.

Bellah admits that the passions of religious commitment do not always run toward a spirit of tolerance and interfaith harmony. Quite the opposite is often the case. As the rise of strident nationalist religious movements around the world has demonstrated, religious fervor, as Bellah puts it, has "often been used for evil as well as good purposes." Still, Bellah believes that the potency of religious passions can be harnessed for good—by which he means a more inclusive sense of religiosity. Moreover, global society needs this kind of religious zeal. "Only such powerful motivation could make human rights genuinely practical" on a global scale, Bellah insists. And he goes on to point out that every religious tradition contains within it the reverence for life and the appreciation for human dignity that is at the basis of universal human rights—not only Christianity, but also Islam, Judaism, Hinduism, Buddhism, and Chinese religion. The *Analects* of Confucius, Bellah reminds us, states, "all within the four seas are brothers." Buddhism regards all human life (and, for that matter, all animate life) as having within it the Buddha nature. Thus religious traditions are the likely sources for a worldwide appreciation of the universality of the principles underlying human rights.

But how can religious leaders be encouraged to turn the message of religious traditions more clearly in the direction of global humanity and away from narrow xenophobia and self-interest? Early in the paper, Bellah makes the observation that people are never as united as they are in a situation of war, when they bind together in opposition to a common enemy. At a later point in the paper, he returns to the theme of war—or at least great social turmoil—and speculates that it will take an awareness of social, economic, and environmental catastrophes so severe that people will turn to religious insights for condemnation of the selfish policies that led these situations, and then they will unite in what William James once called "the moral equivalence of war."[11] Bellah warns, however, that "anxiety and fear have often fueled extremely regressive movements" and even in a time of catastrophic economic inequality and massively irresponsible inaction in the face of environmental disaster, "there is no certainty" that these crises will "move people in the right direction." Still, Bellah would have been impressed by statements of Pope Francis, in November 2013, that trickle-down economics had led to grave economic injustice and was therefore morally sinful.[12]

Whether statements such as the pope's are the beginning of a common front among religious leaders against the economic and environmental crises of our day is an interesting question, but the very fact of the pope's statement—and the enormous support for his outreach toward the poor and marginalized elements of society—does give some credibility to the possibility of Bellah's assertion that religious traditions can be a basis for a sense of transnational stewardship and the moral commitment to a global civil society. Bellah concludes his paper by saying that he is convinced that "religious motivation is a necessary factor" in transforming the growing moral consensus into effective forms of civil society. He envisions the possibility of world law and global governance that will be created in response to an "actually existing global civil society" that has "a spiritual dimension drawing from all the great religions of the world."

DO RELIGION AND CIVIL SOCIETY
NEED EACH OTHER?

Perhaps the most original part of Bellah's contribution to our project is the idea that traditional religions and the emerging global civil society exist in a kind of reciprocal relationship. Much of his thinking about global civil society is not completely novel—as Bellah mentioned, Jürgen Habermas has been thinking about the public sphere and its relationship to both nationalism and transnationalism for some time. In recent years there has also been a wide and growing discussion about the possibilities of a global civil society focused around "cosmopolitanism"—the notion of a shared sense of global citizenship. The pronouncement that at this moment, early in the twenty-first century and in the era of globalization, we are entering into a cosmopolitan age was forcefully made by Kwame Anthony Appiah in his book *Cosmopolitanism: Ethics in a World of Strangers*.[13] Appiah, a scholar of Ghanaian and British background, thinks in terms of a shared global ethic. It is a theme that has been elaborated by Ulrich Beck in *Cosmopolitan Vision* and Giles Gunn in *Ideas to Die For: The Cosmopolitan Challenge*.[14]

The conversations about cosmopolitanism do not talk much about the role of religion, however, and this is where Bellah makes a strong point. Though here too, others have discussed this dimension of global society. Richard Falk, in his book *On Humane Governance: Toward a New Global Politics*, argued in 1995 that religion is "an antidote to the homogenizing impacts of the false universalism and runaway consumerism associated with a new post-Marxist economism."[15] Though Falk is hardly a pious fundamentalist, he sees the value of religious culture in building the moral basis for an enduring world order.[16] The book has recently been updated under the title *(Re) Imagining a Humane Global Governance.*[17]

Another project exploring these issues led to the volume *Religion in Global Civil Society,* which contains essays relating the two concepts, religion and global civil society.[18] The project was directed and the book edited by one of the authors of this book, and it begins with a thoughtful essay by the sociologist Peter Berger on the notion of global civil society. *Religion in Global Civil Society* ends with a remarkably futuristic essay by the political scientist Susanne Rudolph on the possibilities of a transnational religion in the future.[19] So Bellah's interest in the role of religion in global civil society has had precedents.

Still, Bellah has made an original contribution to the discussion, and what is most novel about his thinking is the idea that global civil society and religion need each other. Bellah makes it clear that for global civil society to be grounded in a common moral commitment, it will take more than Immanuel Kant's idea of a universal acceptance of a lowest common denominator of ethical sensitivity or John Rawls's notion of overlapping consensus. Religious traditions provide basic moral concepts and, perhaps more importantly, in Bellah's thinking, the passion and determination to bring these ethical ideals into fruition. At the same time, the health of religious traditions depends on their ability to survive and thrive in the multicultural environment of the modern world. Moreover, it is from the soil of a global civil society that a true global religiosity and common ethic might emerge.

This is an interesting suggestion—that there needs to be a symbiotic relationship between religion and global civil society. But is it the case? In our project, we found considerable evidence that this is so. At the Shanghai workshop, for example, representatives from Indonesia talked about a remarkable effort of several religious traditions to work together on projects for the uplift of Indonesian society. The representatives were part of a training center in the city of Yogyakarta that is supported by Muslim, Hindu, and Christian communities—the three major religious traditions in Indonesian society. They described the diversity of religious traditions in Indonesia as "a major kind of social capital for helping religions or religious communities to work towards a global civil society together."[20]

Discussions around religion's perceived role in fostering civil society were not one-sided, however. Some saw strident nationalist religious elements as an obstacle to civil society, such as James Wellman, who spoke in our workshop on Latin America and the Caribbean about the "structural, cultural relationship between religion and the movement for human security."[21] Wellman saw in religion an expression of people's desire to assure their welfare, human rights, and social freedoms, but it could also become an obstacle to such security when used as a means of political and social exclusion. While religion's oppressive capabilities worried the socialist leaders of the Soviet Union, since its collapse, the promise of security has become a reason to promote the relationship between religion and national civil society. In Russia, religious leaders were conscious of Soviet socialism's attempts to eradicate religion; they saw the need for a religious role in post-Soviet civil society in order to ensure their own survival. Idris Tsechoev, provost at Lomonosov Moscow State University and a participant in the Moscow workshop, suggested that if the various religious communities in his country were not able to coexist and practice their faith peacefully, they would be radicalized and forced underground.[22]

Other participants supported the idea that religion could surmount nationalism and affirmed Bellah's vision of how religious traditions could provide the heart of a global moral community. At the Shanghai workshop, David Palmer, a professor of sociology at the University of Hong Kong, claimed that the religious notions of "oneness and love" provide the possibility for social action. According to him, the essential spiritual principle that is the basis of every religious tradition leads to a desire for justice; it motivates individuals to be critical of the unjust structure of society and "to change the structure of society, to build justice."[23]

At the same time, Mark Woodward, an American scholar who has spent years living in and studying the religious society of Indonesia, warned that the dependent relationship between religion and civil society does not always lead to more openness and tolerance if the dominant religious tradition co-opts the political space of national society. This is what Woodward says has often happened in Indonesia—contradicting some of the other participants' optimistic comments about interfaith cooperation. According to Woodward, the idea of civil society in Indonesia "does not always translate into pluralistic liberal values."[24] Though Woodward is undoubtedly right, the optimistic statements could also be true. The relationship between religion and civil society within a nation—and globally—is complex and sometimes contradictory. Though on a global scale, as Bellah observes, it is also necessary; without religion, the emergent global ethic and civil society will lack spiritual depth.

HOW DO RELIGIOUS GROUPS REACH BEYOND
NARROW RELIGIOUSNESS?

Finding this spiritual depth is not easy. In order for a global civil society with religious underpinnings to emerge, members of religious traditions must spiritually embrace those outside their own faith circle. This means accepting the momentum in the global era to break down boundaries and not defensively protect one's own domain. In the last chapter, we saw how religious creativity in the face of globalization sometimes does lead to the acceptance of multicultural traditions and an openness to shared moral values and spiritual sensibilities. In this chapter, we want to try to understand how this is happening and what aspects of religion will change in the process. Looking for a simple answer to these questions would be futile, though our workshops around the world provided a variety of accounts of faith communities becoming open to alliances and shared concerns with those outside their narrow circles. Taken together, these accounts show that defensiveness is not the only posture toward other religious traditions; there is also a trend toward being more inclusive.

One place this openness is evident is in humanitarian work. Religious organizations have long joined forces with other religious groups and with secular groups to relieve social ills, from poverty to hunger to disease. Thomas Tighe, the head of an NGO—the medical aid organization Direct Relief International—affirmed in our workshop on Latin America and the Caribbean that "religious institutions were the original NGOs."[25] Several of our participants offered ways of understanding the widening concept of humanitarianism in religions. Considering the political battles that can occur over aid to immigrant communities or even welfare to the poorest sectors of a national community, humanitarian religious organizations have to find a way of justifying providing care for those outside their direct purview.

In part, the justification is based on the moral compass that is central to all faiths. Islamic doctrine stresses the importance of taking care of the most vulnerable of the community; Buddhist teachings talk about efforts to alleviate the suffering of all sentient beings everywhere. All faiths have these kinds of precepts. Speaking to the issue of caring for orphans and providing orphanages, Katherine Marshall, senior fellow at Georgetown University's Berkley Center for Religion, Peace, and World Affairs, suggested that religious groups are by far the leaders in tending to the needs of this vulnerable group.[26] In many Western nations, people feel that it is the state that is responsible for such care, but in places such as Cambodia, local communities—and usually religious organizations—take responsibility for these needs.

At our workshop on Southeast Asia, Ria Shibata, a graduate student at Tokyo's Sophia University, noted how some new religious movements in Japan can inspire people on a personal level as well as an organizational level. She described how the Soka Gakkai movement was inspired by the Buddhist ideal of compassion.[27] The movement stressed the need to be compassionate to all, including those outside one's own religious circle. In India, many religious organizations have extended the traditional concept of *seva*—the term for "service," which originally meant serving the gods or the spiritual masters, *gurus,* with offerings—to the notion of social service. Hence the Radhasoami movement, for instance, has created a huge hospital in the Indian state of Punjab that is open to all in need. They are serving not only their own community but also the community of the wider world. The ancient Greeks had a term for such a concept of community: *cosmopolitas,* a "citizen of the cosmos." Hence this impulse toward public service is truly part of a cosmopolitan religion.

A similar impetus inspired Buddhist monks in Cambodia to take a greater role in public life than they had traditionally. In places like Tibet, the *sangha* (community of Buddhist monks) has evolved to become more central in the civil life of the towns within which they were located. The monasteries served as the center for education and legal mediation and guidance on top of being a place of spiritual advancement. Traditionally, their purview was primarily, but not solely spiritual. But as their role has evolved they have become public servants to the whole community, regardless of religious affiliation.

The monastic corps in Cambodia also serves the wider public in several ways, two of which were described by Katherine Marshall in our workshop on South and Southeast Asia. One was their work spreading awareness and support for people afflicted with HIV/AIDS, often in conjunction with UNICEF.[28] The second was regarding environmental protection; the monks are working with a California company to track deforestation. "They actually have monks running around with GPSs to try and monitor whether or not the forests are being cut," Marshall explained.[29] Interestingly, humanitarian work seems to have overshadowed traditional religious education among many of the young monks in Cambodia. According to Marshall, "the general sense is that these young monks don't even begin to understand Buddhism, much less have any direction."[30]

Religious organizations have also begun to lend money, usually on a fairly small scale and largely to help poor communities develop themselves. Microloans, small amounts with low rates of interest, are provided to promising entrepreneurs who lack startup funds. A participant in our workshop on Latin America and the Caribbean, Mary Becker, who is a national board member of Haiti's largest microfinance institution, Fonkoze USA, suggests religion's views of social justice have likely led to a feeling of solidarity with the poor, which informs these growing lending practices.[31] Fonkoze was started in 1994 by a Haitian priest, Father Joseph Philippe, who was inspired by his Christian faith to empower women, whom he saw as the *poto mitan,* the "backbone" of Haiti's economy.[32]

In addition to these long-term development projects, humanitarian religious groups are also ready to act after disasters, be they earthquakes, tsunamis, plague, famine, civil war, or even a sudden economic depression. In such situations, religious communities are often the first to provide aid, in part because, in most cases, they are already on the scene. This was the point made by a participant in our Delhi workshop, Anindita Chakrabarti, professor of sociology at the India Institute of Technology in Kanpur, who spoke specifically about faith-based organizations in India.[33] Some observers alleged, such as Pralay Kanungo professor and chairperson of the Centre for Political Studies, Jawaharlal Nehru University, at our Delhi workshop, that religious humanitarianism is, in fact, "a kind of sectarian humanitarianism," since it "privileges members of the faith community of the donors."[34] Other participants, including representatives of faith-based groups such as Catholic Relief Services and Islamic Relief. insisted that religious aid is given to anyone in need.

In some cases, religious aid workers have sought support from secular agencies. Victoria Riskin, a member of the national board of Human Rights Watch, who participated in our Latin America and Caribbean workshop, described how some local Catholic aid workers in Mexico had come to Human Rights Watch for assistance in issues that the church did not want to address, such as abortion rights for victims of rape and incest. These Catholic women were willing to seek out international NGO support even though the work they were doing was against the church's doctrines.[35]

Something similar was seen to be at work in the Tablighi Jamaat communities of Bangladesh. According to a participant in our Delhi workshop, Rowena Robinson, professor at the Center for the Study of Social Systems in Jawaharlal Nehru University, Tablighi Jamaat, an Islamic group, seeks to bear witness to its religious standards through its work with civil society.[36]

Rather than preach about the teachings that can change lives, members of Tablighi Jamaat serve as living examples of those teachings. They hope that others will emulate their good works, contributing to what Robinson calls "a slow, gradual process of social transformation."[37]

Similar examples of this idea are found in Christianity. The standards of Christian charity provided by figures such as the Albanian nun Mother Teresa, who worked for years among the poor in Calcutta, are sources of inspiration for others to heed the call to help the less fortunate. A participant in our Delhi workshop, Fr. John Chathanatt, principal of the Vidyajyoti College of Theology, called these "foundational experiences," interactions with other people that result in a change in ourselves.[38] Chathanatt proposed that such a transformation of self has had three distinct, but related, levels of change: the attitudinal, by which he meant our attitudes toward others, both inside and outside of our own social group; the behavioral, which accords with how we actually relate to and interact with others; and the cognitional, which looks to the mental processes themselves as a point of change.[39]

India might be a particularly appropriate place to look at how the *practice* of religion in the world is as important as (or more than) *beliefs*. Hinduism never had the central core of doctrine and practices that characterizes other global faiths like Christianity or Islam. The term *Hinduism* is ultimately an umbrella concept that is applied to the myriad forms of religious practice and belief that existed in the lands of India prior to the twentieth century. Moreover, belief itself was often not central. Most scholars of Indian religion would agree with the characterization given by religious studies scholar Catherine Bell, that "Hinduism for Hindus is not a coherent belief system but, first and foremost, a collection of practices."[40] As one of the authors of this book discovered in his early years of field research in India, there is no single term in any Indian language for what Christians and Westerners call "religion."[41]

If India and Southeast Asia provide such examples that challenge the conceptual boundaries about and among religions, they can also demonstrate another boundary that has too often been taken for granted in studies of religion, between religion and so-called secular society. The secular has traditionally been understood as the domain of the state and negatively understood as the absence of religion. It is a reactive term, one that has recently enjoyed a great deal of analysis.[42] As we mentioned in the first chapter of this book, such analysis has challenged the notion that there is a firm distinction between religion and the secular state. Robert Bellah's notion of civil religion shows that national societies, for instances, are not as secular as they might be proclaimed to be.

Talal Asad, the anthropologist who brought about one of the most significant paradigm shifts in how we understand religion in his *Genealogies of Religion,* showed how the realm of the secular is a distinctly modern European notion, which was formed through the exclusion of religion from the realm of power.[43] That realm was made exclusive for the nation-state by excluding religion's voice, and Asad examines how the history of Western Christianity led to the creation of such a space. Nations in which Islam was predominant, Asad notes, took a different turn.

The notion of a separate, secular sphere that came out of the West also had repercussions on how Western societies viewed religion: as something separate from public life and separate from politics. It is no surprise, then, that a comparative analysis of non-Western cultures—be they Middle Eastern, African, or Asian—had trouble understanding how religion worked in cultures where the lines between religion and secular were blurred. It took a global perspective to challenge such assumptions.

At our Delhi workshop, I. A. Rehman offered such a perspective when he reflected on the multiple identities that are blended in Indian culture. "Motilal Nehru, father of Jawaharlal Nehru (India's first prime minister), could declare at a public meeting that 'I am a Kashmiri *pandit* [part of the Brahmin community from the Kashmir valley], a Hindu, but a Kachari Muslim,'" and then he added that it is possible that we can "have a religious experience, and we can all be secular in politics."[44] Identities do not only come in two kinds, religious or secular. They run the gamut between them, often integrating aspects we may label "political" or "spiritual."

At the same time that members of religious communities are redefining the boundaries between faiths and between religion and the secular, secular service groups are also reaching out, connecting with their religious partners in mutual projects. By "secular," in this context, we simply mean groups such as Human Rights Watch and UNESCO, which do not have a specific religious connection. NGOs that are not bolstered by faith or doctrine face many of the issues that faith-based humanitarian organizations confront, such as identifying who will benefit from their services and how best to get aid to disparate communities. On the whole, the secular solutions seem to be the same as the religious ones: to go where the need is the greatest.

For this reason, some secular groups regularly work with faith-based relief workers in the field. Direct Relief International (DRI), which provides donated medical supplies around the world, often partners with religious humanitarian groups in order to distribute their materials. According to DRI's CEO, Thomas Tighe, his organization chooses what groups to work with primarily based on their perceived effectiveness—that is, whether or not they can get the job done.[45] Religious groups have proven to be very effective. Tighe wondered aloud whether this meant that when his organization reaches out to provide medical supplies to desperate people in Muslim areas of the African Sahara, it was unknowingly and unintentionally advancing a religious program.[46] The answer to his question lies in the perceptions of the Saharan recipients of the aid, whether they see these medical supplies as simply the generosity of wealthier people or as covert attempts to lure the needy into the donors' way of life.

Despite these questions, however, there appears to be a symbiosis of common endeavor that unite both religious and secular humanitarian organizations. This brings us back to the spirit of our Buenos Aires workshop, where animated conversations about social concerns could be conducted without any reference to the faith—or the lack of it—of the speakers. But as Robert Bellah has pointed out, this shared moral discourse has roots in a common worldview, an emerging global civil society. What is intriguing is Bellah's suggestion that, like the civil religion of national societies, global civil society has a shared spirituality as well as a shared morality. By this we simply mean a sensibility about basic values and what the theologian Paul Tillich called "ultimate concerns." But because the philosopher Michel Foucault, among others, has taught us that social concepts reflect alignments of social power, we need to consider whether there are aspects of what are professed to be common assumptions that, in fact, privilege some over others. We still wonder what is in the mind of the Saharan recipient of medical aid from the U.S.-based Direct Relief International. In other words, we need to address the question of how global are the values of global civil society. It is to this question that we now turn.

Orthodox priest, Moscow. Photograph by Dinah Griego.

FIVE

The Annoying Certainty
of Global Views

THE DANGERS OF CULTURAL IMPERIALISM

ONE OF THE MORE DRAMATIC moments in our discussions began calmly enough. We had gathered in Santa Barbara with a group of scholars and activists who were involved in, or were knowledgeable about, the current religious situation in northern Africa and the Middle East. Among the participants were Middle Eastern Muslims and African Muslims and Christians, as well as Americans, most from a European ethnic background, who were familiar with the region. The topic had turned to human rights and the role that religion could play either in supporting or obstructing human-rights policies.

Two of the American participants, a couple who had worked with an NGO in Ghana, began to warm up to a matter that clearly troubled them. The treatment of gay people, the wife announced, is the greatest human-rights crime of North Africa and the Middle East. Her husband was quick to agree. They regarded it as something akin to female genital mutilation— the so-called female circumcision. Clearly the time had come for concerned citizens to take a stand on the persecution of gays and lesbians as well.[1]

There was a noticeable silence for a few minutes, and the conversation wandered off in other directions. Several of us were looking nervously around the room, wondering whether the issue would be ignored or challenged. Our fear was that it would provoke a defensive reaction.

It did. The first response came from a Muslim scholar from Egypt who took the soft approach. He said that most Muslims took a "don't ask, don't tell" approach to the matter, that there were a diversity of positions, and that religious leaders were doing a pretty good job of trying to keep the worst excesses of discrimination against gay and lesbian people from occurring, even though, he implied, he personally regarded homosexuality as an aberration.[2]

Another Muslim participant implied that attitudes were changing in the Islamic world on this issue but that outside influence often made matters worse.

This was not enough for the American couple, however, who pressed on. They challenged the notion that religious leaders were neutral on the issue and told a story about a high official in the Presbyterian Church in Ghana, a man of great intellectual stature, whom otherwise they respected, who proclaimed homosexual behavior a sin and threatened to break off relations with the more moderate Presbyterian Church in America over this issue.[3] They regarded this as shameful; the church should be on the forefront of liberation, they implied.

We all held our breath as the conversation wandered in other directions again, but soon the Egyptian came back to the topic. He explained very simply that this was not a matter of human rights, since same-sex activity was clearly sinful and against the laws of God and nature. He launched into his own theological insights on the subject, comparing the position in the Qur'an as similar to the notion of yin and yang in the Chinese Taoist tradition. There is a male force and a female force, and the Qur'an affirms that the natural order of things is for men and women to couple, he said.[4] He thought that this issue was qualitatively different from female genital mutilation, a matter that he claimed was against the laws of Qur'an—though this interpretation is not universally accepted—but, he claimed, homosexuality was different. It was clearly un-Islamic and unnatural and unacceptable. For him, this was the end of the story.

Again there was a silence; people genuinely didn't know what to say. Among the Americans at the workshop, there was probably not a single one of us who took this line of thinking. Like most progressive Westerners, we regarded homosexuality as nothing more than a normal variation in the complex variety of sexual attitudes and types in the human psychological makeup. Moreover, we shuddered to think of those poor gay Ghanaians, Nigerians, or Egyptians having to cower under such cultural condemnation, which produces closeted secrecy at best, depression and ostracism at worst.

During the break after the session, one of the discussion leaders tried to smooth things over by suggesting to the quarreling parties that there are many different perspectives on this issue, and religious people of all stripes can disagree. He mentioned how his own Episcopal church has been torn apart worldwide by this issue, with most American Episcopal congregations accepting the membership of LGBT people and even the ordination of gay and lesbian clergy, and most African Episcopal Church leaders denouncing both homosexuality and the American church's tolerance toward it. He might have added, but didn't, that the local church he attended had just proudly hosted a visit from the new bishop of the Episcopal Diocese of Southern California, who was the first openly lesbian cleric to be installed into this high leadership role anywhere in the Episcopal worldwide communion. She was such a nice person, he wanted to say; why would anyone bother with something that most of the parishioners in the church thought was irrelevant to her qualifications as a bishop, the issue of her sexuality?

But he didn't say this. Perhaps it was a lack of moral courage. But it was also a matter of wanting to avoid the larger question—when it comes to universal values, whose values are more universal than others? After all, the Middle East Muslim and the Nigerian Christian regarded their points of view as normal and universal as we felt that ours were. One of the other Muslim participants in the seminar had made that point rather specifically. Though he was sympathetic with our position, he said that outside pressure on the issue of homosexuality "could do more harm than good," since it was seen by many in Africa and the Middle East as a kind of "colonial ploy."[5]

The same kind of ethical standoff occurred in a similarly tense moment in Moscow. Again, it was over homosexuality. In this case, however, we were the ones who sparked the discussion—inadvertently, in a sense, because what we were trying to ask was whether contemporary American assumptions about what were normal aspects of human rights could be regarded as a kind of domineering moralism. The example we gave was the U.S. State Department's announcement that considerations of American aid would be based, in part, on human-rights considerations. And from the American point of view, these human rights extended to the freedom of gay and lesbian people. We politely referred to this policy in wondering whether in other parts of the world, where cultural assumptions are different, this could be taken as a culturally arrogant issue.

Well. The priest from the Russian Orthodox Church visibly stiffened, tilting his bearded face forward and roared, "this is not a matter of cultural difference." Turning to look at each of us around the seminar table, he pronounced, "homosexuality is simply sin."[6]

He was quickly joined by several of his colleagues, including some of the professors from Moscow State University, who tried to adopt a more moderate tone. They affirmed that yes, homosexuality was a sin, but one could try to be as hospitable as possible to those afflicted with the condition. A few participants appeared clearly uncomfortable with this accommodation to civility, however, and one began to describe several conspiracy theories he had heard about how the American CIA, in collaboration with UNESCO, was setting up training camps in Latin America and elsewhere to seduce hapless young people into the homosexual "lifestyle."[7]

The Americans present were astonished at this line of reasoning and were eager to bring the conversation back to what they regarded as a more sensible exchange of views. The discussion leader tried to repeat the old line about how Christians could disagree about many things, including this one, but clearly the priest was having none of it. This issue had obviously been hotly debated in Russian society, and the raw nerves associated with it were barely beneath the surface of polite conversation, ready to be inflamed by any mention of the topic.

In the end, we returned to the issue that had propelled us into the conversation in the first place: the idea that one society's understanding of the universality of human rights could be taken by other societies as a form of cultural domination. There was no need to dwell on that conclusion, however, since the tense encounter was an abundant illustration of the problem.

During the break, when we were all collecting our breath, a young Russian student who had been sitting silently at the perimeter of the room came up to us and whispered, "don't take this as typical of all of us." He added, "we in the younger generation see things differently; we're more like you."

We appreciated the affirmation, and yet his comments gave us even more food for thought. Did it illustrate the point that the Russian Orthodox priest was making, that the openness to homosexuality was a Western attitude—a perversion, from his point of view—that was infecting the youth of his country, and for this reason they needed to be adamant in opposing it? In trying to put ourselves into his shoes, we could see that the priest would cheerfully welcome the law that had been recently passed by the Russian parliament and enthusiastically endorsed by President Vladimir Putin, the law that banned what it called the distribution of "propaganda of nontraditional sexual relations to minors." This meant that the state outlawed anything that encouraged acceptance of homosexuality and made illegal any public statements that referred to this kind of sexual orientation as normal.

How odd this seemed to us Americans. And yet we knew many people in our own country who might agree with the law, and we knew that there was no such thing as 100 percent consensus on any moral issue. The ethical approval of abortions, for instance, and the easy availability of contraceptive devices are among those other contentious moral issues that divide well-meaning persons. But recognizing those divisions and knowing what to do about them are two different matters. To capitulate fully to the notion of cultural diversity in moral matters means accepting a kind of moral relativism in the world that would make any hope of a global civil society and the moral and spiritual elements of a global religion impossible. The cosmopolitan dream would be a myth. Hence it is vital to affirm that there are some moral absolutes when it comes to a perspective for the dignity of all life and the protection of the rights of all people. And yet how do we determine which values and rights are authentically universal and which are simply products of our own narrow cultural perspectives?

ARE HUMAN VALUES UNIVERSAL?

In Russia we had to be careful with issues regarding homosexuality—just as we did in conversation with African and Middle Eastern participants. In China, however, the sensitive issue was regions that they regarded as separatist. Tibet and the Uighur region were the most touchy topics. What many Americans regard as the human rights of Tibetan Buddhists and Uighur Muslims to express their yearning for cultural freedom are seen by many Chinese—probably most of them—as instances of antinationalist separatism. It's ironic that the Dalai Lama, the Tibetan spiritual leader (and, until 2011, political leader in exile), is himself a global phenomenon, speaking in support of the very kinds of universal values we are seeking here. For China, however, His Holiness the Dalai Lama is not a symbol of brotherhood across borders; he is the leader of a political movement seeking independence for the Tibetan people.

Consider how Americans would feel if Hawaii suddenly wanted to regain its autonomy, a freedom that was lost in 1893 with the overthrow of the independent regime led by Queen Lili'uokalani. Though most people in Hawaii are proud of the native Hawaiian cultural heritage of the state, there is uneasiness about the Hawaiian sovereignty movement, with its suggestion that the current state administration is intrinsically illegitimate. An outright secessionist movement would likely be banned. And though the parallels between Hawaii and Tibet are by no means exact, it is fair to say that most Chinese think of Tibet as being as firmly a part of contemporary China as Hawaii is of the United States, and that any Chinese person has a right to live and conduct business there.[8] Thus, though all of us—Chinese and Americans—might affirm the right to a free expression of religious culture and belief, we might have vastly different ways of thinking about that expression when issues of political power, identity, and sovereignty are involved.

The Russian attitude toward gays is, in our view, more problematic. In an attempt to reconcile our two positions, one of the Russian participants in Moscow explained the matter this way: he said they agreed with us that there is a human right for individuals to do whatever they wanted to do—in private. "I may have a negative or a positive attitude towards someone," the Russian professor said, "but I have no right to touch him, and so I must let him do what he pleases," as long as it does not disturb other people or interfere with their liberty. "However," he added, "when people impose their norms and lifestyle by demonstrating them on parades, then it becomes an element of propaganda, and it is an entirely different matter."[9] In other words, he was arguing that social mores needed to be protected. But then he added that the situation was complicated by the fact that the cultural values expressed in the gay-rights parades were not just atypical in Russian culture, they were imports of "a foreign culture into another culture." For this reason, he regarded the gay-rights movement in Russia as a kind of foreign aggression.

Our feeling is that the rights of individuals to express their sexual orientation in public is a fundamental human right—everywhere, in all cultures, and at all times. In our view, it is a matter of accepting the natural differences of the human condition, and it is as wrong to discriminate on the basis of sexual orientation as it is to reject people because of the color of their skin or whether they are right-handed or left-handed. And by the way, throughout history, left-handed people have been ostracized for their "difference." Our language still conveys elements of earlier prejudices against them: we think of someone mysteriously evil as "sinister," from the Latin *sinistra,* "left"; and the French term for "left," *gauche,* is the term we use for anyone who is crude or socially clumsy. Today, of course, we would recoil with horror if people around the world were mistreated simply because they were left-handed. We feel the same way about sexual orientation.

But not everyone thinks the way we do, and this is the problem. It is a problem for us as individuals, since we would like to think that our values are universal human values. But it is also a problem for our understanding of global civil society, since we need to be assured that there is a common repository of human values that are shared throughout the planet. We don't want to imagine that the only way to achieve a common global ethic is through coercion or by cultural domination.

Yet it is difficult to do anything on unfamiliar cultural soil without bring-ing along the baggage of our own culturally shaped assumptions about what is right. One of the authors of this book discovered this in a direct way years ago, when he first lived in India, in a row house in a middle-class neighbor-hood near the university where he was studying. His neighbors, he observed, all hired this same bedraggled family of sweepers to clean their houses, one after the other, at least once a week. Of course, he was used to cleaning his own house—or at least as much as a young man in his twenties is capable of cleaning anything—and was determined to show them how an egalitarian society, such as the American one from which he had come, had no use for servants. We could manage household cleaning on our own. All were equal.

But this was not the message that his neighbors received. One of them knocked on his door one afternoon and wanted to have a little talk. The neighbors were talking, he said, about his lack of servants and the fact that the American was doing his own cleaning.

"Yes," the American student said brightly, thinking that they had gotten his egalitarian point.

"We are all disappointed with you," he said, saying that obviously the American was rich—he was an American, after all, student or not—but he refused to relinquish a few rupees for the poor sweepers, who were willing to work for a pittance. "Surely," he said, "you have it within your heart to do the right thing and give those poor people some simple employment."

So our cultural values are not always conveyed in the way that we would like them to be. Our good intentions often backfire or are misunderstood. In one of our workshops, a representative of the international humanitarian organization World Vision spoke about the difficulties she and her colleagues encountered in providing relief supplies and monetary aid to desperate villages in famine-ridden Africa. They had intended to put the villagers back on their feet and make it possible for them to be self-sustaining again. But they discov-ered that the easy availability of their relief supplies and monetary aid was creating a culture of dependency. Their good motivations had turned into something unexpected and unwanted. Eventually they shifted to a different model of aid that involved payment in food and money for development projects that the villagers would create on their own. According to the World Vision representative at our workshop, "the whole purpose" of the aid pro-gram was shifted in order "to empower the community to be sustainable."[10]

NGO aid resulting in a culture of dependency was also an issue in Bangladesh, according to Lamia Karim. The surge in institutions supporting microfinancing loans brought over two thousand NGO representatives into Bangladesh, all hoping to enable development, empower women entrepreneurs, and encourage overall economic growth. The result was a surprise. With the huge number of establishments bringing resources into the country, the Bangladeshi government basically outsourced state functions—education, health care, and the like—to NGOs. The administration judged that these foreign organizations were better equipped to provide these services, so it just handed them over. Not only did this reduce the ability of the state to be the primary institution for the care of its citizens, but also, according to Karim, it prevented the full political engagement of the communities where the NGOs were active.[11]

These cases of the unforeseen consequence of humanitarian aid are problematic, but they do not reveal a clash of values—or do they? Is there a utilitarian drive to Western relief efforts that consistently skew humanitarian efforts to results, defined in a narrow, materialist way, as opposed to community development? This was the question raised by Delhi workshop participant Ranjana Mukhopadhyaya. She said that providing aid to people in need is important, but "more important are the kinds of ideology that are being generated" in "these kinds of transformative movements," whether it is feeding the hungry or empowering women through microcredit schemes.[12] She had a couple concerns: receiving aid or money without earning it is a problematic social lesson to impart; and relying upon international agencies rather than the domestic network of development assistance can be seen as undercutting the social network and usurping the gains made by civil society.

Concern about the ideology of foreign aid organizations is likely what caused the Islamist backlash against international NGOs in Egypt, according to Samah Khalil Faried in our Cairo workshop. Faried, a lecturer in sociology at Ain Shams University in Cairo, noted that people in Egypt seemed opposed to what she called the "new patterns of NGOs,"[13] which rely on outside funding for their ability to engage with the state. These organizations have no constituency of local agents and are perceived by many to be a channel for foreign influence into Egyptian politics, leading to a great deal of resistance by both popular Islamist groups and also their opponents, the Egyptian Supreme Council of Military Forces. The problem was not that the international groups were offering (much needed) aid but that the ideology supporting the aid was considered "foreign" and opposed to the idea of Egypt that these groups maintained.

In his response to Faried's comment, Amr Abdulrahman analyzed the complex relationship Egyptian governments have had with foreign powers.[14] Egypt has a complicated past with outside influence on their government, he said, and it is a past shared by many countries in North Africa and the Middle East. The culture of dependency that World Vision was concerned about above has this other face, the blowback against too much reliance on and influence from those outside the community.

Countries like Cambodia, Mozambique, and Ethiopia were suggested as illustrations of how the images of international NGOs can be damaged by the way they have addressed various crises. NGOs moved into Cambodia during a period of political upheaval, when the central government was unable to provide for its citizens, but the NGO's efforts went haywire, according to Katherine Marshall. As the situation for Cambodians improved and violence waned, the NGOs swept in with a great deal of resources for education, health services, and other forms of aid. As the government slowly regained power and tried to implement its own programs in these sectors, they clashed with those that the NGOs set up, and Cambodian citizens were caught in the middle.[15]

At our Delhi workshop, Richard Falk provided some historical context for the ways that current ideologies can affect what kind of aid is "good" or "bad." For years, Falk was the Milbank Professor of International Law at Princeton, and is now a fellow of the Orfalea Center at the University of California at Santa Barbara. He related how the global discussion during the Cold War was dominated by the competition between societies that were culturally religious and those observing a state-sponsored atheism. For the "religious" states, which were the home of most of the international NGOs, including the faith-based NGOs, any group opposed to communism and Marxism was good. According to Falk, this applied to Muslim charitable organizations as well as Christian ones: "the huge financing of madrasahs in the region by Salafi and Wahhabi elements of Islam, particularly based in Saudi Arabia, were viewed with a kind of favor" in an ideological climate where "anti-Communism was more important than anything else."[16]

In a post-Cold War world, we no longer divide the world into religious versus atheist. Russian authorities now rely on the Russian Orthodox Church for much of their cultural support, and China tolerates the open adherence to the world's major religious faiths and has embraced Confucianism as a kind of state religion. So there is not an ideological bias regarding religion. But there is one toward human rights.

One of the greatest areas of misunderstanding in the world today is between countries that ascribe to the idea that there are universal human rights and countries that think that their cultural and political traditions are exceptions. The bias of Western humanitarian organizations is toward the idea of universal human rights. A participant in our Buenos Aires workshop, Carlos Escude, then director of the Centro de Estudios Internacionales y de Educacion para la Globalizacion at the Universidad del Cema, stated that the very language of universal human rights can be the new means of dividing the world. The concept has dominated global conversations about ethics since Eleanor Roosevelt helped pen the Universal Declaration of Human Rights (UDHR) in the 1940s, with the implication that countries that recognize these rights as universal are somehow better, and those that do not accept it are less morally developed. When the United Nations was being established and the UDHR was being debated, several countries disagreed with the focus that European countries placed on human rights, including China and Saudi Arabia.

China's complaint about universal human rights was that it might hamper the country's economic development; it worried that the standards imposed by the UDHR would derail their ability to develop their resources.[17] The limits placed on hours and working conditions were not conducive to China's developmental needs and the timeline it envisioned. Saudi Arabia's problems, on the other hand, were based in their interpretation of Islamic doctrines around gender roles. The Wahhabi branch of Islam, which lies at the core of the Saudi Arabian monarchical state and inspired Salafi ideology, saw gender equality as a kind of Western European importation.

When Jamil al-Baroody, the Saudi representative to the UDHR council, offered his remarks in 1947 about the limitations of human rights, he argued that the focus on human rights ultimately imposes upon the world a standard only found in the West. In doing so, the international body used a kind of cultural particularism to speak on a universal level. "It was not for the Commission," al-Baroody said, "to proclaim the superiority of one civilization over all others."[18] Human rights was, and in some places continues to be, seen as a kind of Western imperialism, based in the ideas of the European Enlightenment, forced onto all other civilizations without the awareness that other civilizations might have something of value to add. China and Saudi Arabia are each the inheritors of millennia of cultural tradition, much older than that of the not-yet-two-centuries-old United States that led the discussion on the UDHR. The message sent by both countries was perhaps best formulated by al-Baroody: the United Nations needed to stop "ignoring more ancient civilizations that are past the experimental stage."[19]

But if human rights are not universal, how can there be a global ethic to undergird the emerging global civil society? How do we allow for the wide variety of values, religious and secular, of different civilizations around the globe without reverting to moral relativism? If something as basic to us in the West as human rights cannot provide a base, what can? Carlos Escude averred that he yearned for a global civil society, but only one built on basic human rights. He said he could accept the concept of global civil society only if it were "anchored on the idea that all men and women are created equal."[20]

THE DANGERS OF CULTURAL IMPERIALISM

These issues do not have easy solutions. Often the frustration with finding a solution leads to a desire to brush aside such concerns and simply get down to the work that needs to be done. Where there is poverty, sponsor development. Where there is oppression, support democratic movements. Find the problems and just get in there to help out; let the ideological niceties follow. As we noted earlier, however, this utilitarian attitude is itself a value judgment that can be seen as offensive.

At our Africa and Middle East workshop, Fritz Lampe, an anthropologist at Northern Arizona University, reflected on his experiences in Africa. He asked whether we in the West can just walk into the continent and assume we know what in African society needs to be developed and by whom. He wondered whether "we are reflecting our own cultural bias" when we do not start with local perspectives.[21] Lampe's point was that the identification of where aid should be distributed stems from a certain ideal of what culture *should* look like. To get around that prejudice, we have to take seriously the perspectives and cultural values of local communities.

But must we accept all of these cultural values? Few Westerners would justify female genital mutilation, which is politely called "female circumcision." Few of us tolerate societies where privilege is allocated on the basis of race, caste, or family status. But despite this diversity of viewpoints, most of us feel that there are basic aspects of human dignity that should be universal. Many of us tend to agree with Carlos Escude's point, that a global civil society has to be based on such fundamental rights as gender equality. But what about societies that have a different view of male-female relations? And what about other issues, such as the rights of people with diverse sexual orienta-tions? Is our insistence on all of the rights that we admire a form of cultural imperialism? Many in the West cannot recall the colonial past when the white man's opinion was the law, but those memories linger in areas of the world that suffered the brunt of earlier attempts to create a global society of colonialism. Without reflection into the ways our own cultural biases inform our worldview, we risk committing the same mistakes, however well meaning.

Religious entrepreneurs have had a long tradition of taking part in such imperial projects, both on behalf of the political state and in their own hopes to gain adherents. In North America, Christian missionaries accompanied settlers pushing westward into the lands that they regarded as uninhabited, but where, in fact, a great number of American Indian tribes had long lived. A certain religious sentiment and character became part of what it meant to be "civilized," and being "civilized" became a prerequisite for recognition in the political and legal structure of the growing United States. The result was the decimation of entire Native American cultures.[22]

Many places around the world still worry about these kinds of conse-quences that come with religious belief. China, for example, has held mis-sionaries at arm's length since the Jesuit Matteo Ricci founded the missionary effort in China in the sixteenth century, and Christian proselytizing remains outlawed in the country. But Christian groups are welcomed into the coun-try when they carry aid in the wake of natural disasters. Following the 2008 earthquake in China's Sichuan province, Christian aid workers were allowed into the country only on the promise that no missionary work was to be done.[23] As Katherine Marshall put it, in a global era, it has become generally accepted that "proselytization or linking or conditionality in humanitarian relief situations is both illegal and unethical."[24] By "linking or conditional-ity," Marshall means linking aid to religious affiliation or giving aid on the condition that someone will convert.

Still, faith-based humanitarian organizations are often suspected of hav-ing a hidden agenda to try to convert the recipients of their aid. In Indonesia, for example, following the 2004 Indian Ocean tsunami, many organizations were accused of spreading their faith under the cover of aid. According to Elizabeth Collins, a participant in our South and Southeast Asia workshop who served as the director of two humanitarian projects in Indonesia, certain Christian humanitarian groups were accused of aggressively and secretively proselytizing under the auspices of providing aid, and an ongoing reaction against so-called Christianization has continued in the archipelago.[25] According to Fernando Lopez-Alves, who participated in our Buenos Aires workshop, some local Christian churches try to infiltrate secular NGOs in order to proselytize. According to Lopez-Alves, they were told to "just be anonymous" and work with the secular NGO, and when they provided aid to people they were supposed to "try to convince them to become Christians."[26]

But not all missionary activity is Christian. And Christians are not the only religious people who have provided pious inducements along with their humanitarian aid. Extremist Muslim groups have done the same thing. Hizbollah in Lebanon and Hamas in Palestine operate large charitable operations, often with a Muslim message attached. According to Mary Zurbuchen, "some of these groups are vociferously intolerant of other faiths and even within Islam promote an anti-pluralist agenda." She had in mind African groups with a Salafi Islamist point of view. Missionaries from these groups enter conflict areas and provide aid along with a hardline message. In some cases they follow the path of Christian evangelical missionaries and criticize as encouraging apostasy any attempt of the Christians to score converts but then end up gaining converts themselves on behalf of their extreme Muslim ideology. In this way, according to Zurbuchen, "they recruit new members who are, perhaps, from a less hardline background."[27]

Although most of the evangelizing that accompanies humanitarian aid is religious, Mark Woodward pointed out in our South and Southeast Asia workshop that any attempt to inflict one's values on another culture can be seen as a kind of proselytizing. It is possible to imagine a kind of secular proselytizing, requiring, for example, that recipients of aid ascribe to Western norms of human rights, such as gender equality. The promotion of "Western secular feminist" ideals, according to Woodward, appears to be just as much a missionary activity as actions by evangelical Christians, and, he added, "in many cases, this is deeply resented by Islamic feminists."[28]

As Richard Falk noted in our workshop on Africa and the Middle East, humanitarian institutions have been used as agents for political propaganda for years. Falk shared a story about how the United Nations has been seen, at times, as an agent of the West and has suffered for it. In March 2003, the U.S. military, along with coalition forces, invaded Iraq. Many nations opposed the invasion, as did many people in the United States, Britain, and Australia, whose governments led the charge, in part because it would create a humanitarian crisis within the country. Five months later, to help coordinate UN relief efforts and provide a neutral space for contesting groups in Iraq to come together peaceably, the United Nations established the United Nations Assistance Mission for Iraq (UNAMI).[29] One of the United Nation's top diplomats, Special Representative Sérgio Vieira de Mello, was sent to Baghdad to provide a benign UN presence in the midst of crisis. The Brazilian diplomat had a long career in UN service and was rumored to be a likely candidate to be the next secretary general of the organization.

Only five days after the creation of UNAMI, Sérgio Vieira de Mello was dead, along with twenty-two others, victims of a suicide bomber who detonated a truck filled with explosives at the headquarters of the UN mission, housed in the old Canal Hotel. The tragedy was followed by another bombing in September, precipitating the withdrawal of all UN staff from the area. While the humanitarian mission failed, the military mission would continue for years, ultimately resulting in a fractured nation that, at the time of this writing, is still experiencing fierce sectarian strife.

The group that would become known as al-Qaeda in Iraq claimed responsibility for the 2003 bombings. In his statement claiming responsibility, Abu Musab al-Zarqawi, the Jordanian extremist who was head of the terrorist organization, bragged that they had destroyed the UN building that was "the protectors of Jews, the friends of the oppressors and aggressors." Zarqawi blamed the United Nations for having "recognized the Americans as the masters of Iraq" and for having given "Palestine as a gift to the Jews so they can rape the land and humiliate our people." He also cited the United Nations' role in what he regarded as the suppression of Muslims in Bosnia, Kashmir, Afghanistan, and Chechnya.[30] In the eyes of al-Qaeda in Iraq the United Nations was not an international body intent on peaceful integration; it was another arm of U.S. policy. According to our workshop participant Richard Falk, who for many years was the UN Human Rights Commission's special rapporteur for Palestine, the United Nations made "a great mistake in Iraq by seeming to be part of the enterprise of American occupation."[31]

It was said that in ancient Rome one could walk the length of the Roman Empire unscathed merely by professing *civis Romanus sum,* "I am a Roman citizen," since no one dared incur the wrath of the empire. Today, it seems that the opposite is the case. Appearing to be aligned with powerful states can be a liability. International NGOs labor to appear autonomous and independent, free from the biases and prejudices of the United States and other large powers. In the words of Richard Falk, they aim "not to be seen, to the extent possible, as the agent of geopolitical forces."[32] Yet the mere adherence to international standards of human rights and reasoned diplomacy can be seen as taking sides with the values of the hegemonic West.

SO WHAT DO WE DO?

We return to the basic problem: how to think globally without imposing ourselves on others. The problems posed in trying to find a consensus on human values to undergird a global civil society can seem hopelessly complex and discouraging. At one point or another, perhaps every participant in our workshops gave a sigh of resignation over this issue. But the discussions also led to some guidelines for moving ahead.

Perhaps the most basic advice was to listen. Several participants underscored how much their own understanding changed when they tried to put themselves empathetically in the place of those from a different cultural background. They tried to listen in a way that illuminated the social and cultural context.

An example of this kind of empathetic understanding was provided at our South and Southeast Asia workshop by Caroline Meyer-White, who works in Pakistan as the project manager for Danish Muslim Aid as well as with Engineers without Borders. She shared the importance of appreciating cultural notions in their particular context, including specific connotations of certain words. Take the madrasah, for example, which is often regarded in the West as an Islamic school providing rote religious learning and training in anti-American attitudes. In the area of Pakistan where Meyer-White worked, however, the term *madrasah* also carries an economic charge and refers especially to schools for poor children. The curriculum is not limited to religion, nor does it necessarily promote political views.[33] The term *Taliban* in the Pakistani context can also be misunderstood. To the Westerner, the term conjures up images of bearded men in mountainous villages who impose strict shari'ah law on their communities. But in the areas of Pakistan where Meyer-White's projects were grounded, the term referred simply to students of Islamic theology, not a particular kind of Muslim. "Caroline," she was told by her Pakistani colleague, "you and me are both Taliban. We both believe that we can create a better world, to have such idealistic beliefs and to study how to reach it is to be a Taliban."[34]

Another guideline for cultural understanding is to gain a local perspective on what kind of aid and development support is needed rather than assume that the outsider already knows what is best. An example of this was given by one of the participants in our Africa and Middle East workshop, Mae Cannon, the senior director of advocacy and outreach for World Vision U.S., a Christian NGO engaged in humanitarian activity around the world. Cannon said that the model should be one of "partnership," a model that can change the conversation from "working *on* a problem to working *with* people to solve the problem."[35]

In a similar vein, the International Association of Black Religions and Spiritualities (IABRS) trains American students to approach international aid work with cultural sensitivity and an openness to learn. According to a participant at our Africa and Middle East workshop, Dwight Hopkins, founder of IABRS and a professor at the University of Chicago Divinity School, it sends students from developed nations to other countries to "learn from the people there."[36] Most participants in our workshops agreed with this approach. They thought that any progress toward a common moral substratum to global civil society must be developed through interaction rather than being assumed or imposed. It has to begin with a willingness to listen and learn from others and to forge common points of understanding.

In one poignant moment, during a break after the rather contentious discussion of homosexuality in Africa and the Middle East that was mentioned at the outset of this chapter, one of the Muslim participants approached us quietly as we lined up for coffee and cookies. "It was a tense session," he admitted. But then he added, "don't push us into a corner; you have to give us time to evolve on these matters." He was hinting at a higher level of moral reconciliation that lay beyond our stated differences. And his voice carried a suggestion of hope that there could be a moral basis to global civil society after all.

Tahrir Square, Cairo. Photograph by Paul Lynch.

Conclusion

GOD IN THE GLOBAL SQUARE

CAIRO'S TAHRIR SQUARE HAS BEEN at the center of the tumultuous changes in recent Egyptian life. As we witnessed when we held our workshop next door to the square and observed the rallies first hand, it was a hub of extraordinary activity, one of those places that the anthropologist Clifford Geertz describes as providing "concentrated loci of serious acts," where "momentous events" are thought to occur.[1] It was a stage on which both space and time were compressed into defining moments. The square encompassed a microcosm of Egyptian society, and the charged atmosphere seemed to bring together both past and future. It exhibited all of the anger and resentment over the repression that had come before, and all of the hopes and aspirations of the society the protestors hoped to build in years to come. The square was alive with possibility; it was a rock concert, a political rally, and a festival of life. And the action continued long after the fall of Mubarak. There were protests at Tahrir after the election that brought the Muslim Brotherhood to power, and further protests when the military cracked down on Islamic organizations, and yet more protests when new elections were called to bring a replacement government into power. In all of these remarkable changes in Egypt, Tahrir Square was in the middle of the action.

Much can be said of other squares that have dominated the headlines in recent years. In Ukraine, Kiev's Independence Square, in the heart of the city, was the scene of a remarkable set of protests in February 2014 that brought down the regime of Russian-supported President Viktor Yanukovych. Popularly known by the Persian term *Maidan*, the square was a microcosm of Ukrainian nationalist communities and a dense center of political interaction and change. In Turkey in 2013, Taksim Square in Istanbul became the locus of a series of protests that ultimately involved an estimated eighty million people across Turkey protesting, among other things, the anti-secular position of Prime Minister Recep Tayyip Erdogan.

Elsewhere in the world, other squares also have been the venues for antiauthoritarian gatherings and social protests. The anticorporate Occupy Movement that swept the world in 2011 and 2012 began in Zuccotti Park near New York City's Wall Street financial district. As the movement's name implied, it involved the occupation of scores of public parks and squares from Oakland to Madrid, from South Africa to South America. For weeks and months, protestors concerned about the mounting inequalities in the world's economic distribution camped out in these public spaces, claiming them for their alternative vision of society.

Years earlier, on June 4 in 1989, in China, a protest movement made an enduring impact on China's political life. Heady with the possibilities of change in the post-Cold War era, as China opened itself economically to the world, thousands of young protestors gathered in Beijing's Tiananmen Square to demand democratic change and more personal freedoms. The Tiananmen protests were crushed, and references to the event have been excised from China's official memory—including even internet search engines and reference works. But the memories and the spirit of the movement lived on. The massive protests in 2009 that ended Iran's Green Revolution, following the unsuccessful bid of the reform candidate Mir-Hossein Mousavi for the presidency, were also brutally smashed by Iran's Islamist regime. And like Tiananmen, the radical spirit of the protest movement in the squares of Tehran lived on to help support reformist leaders in subsequent elections. Not all of the protest gatherings in public squares have led to a demonstrable and immediate change.

Yet the very fact that the protests were held and the symbolism of occupying the public space of a square or park or major intersection mark a distinctive development in the political life of the global era. These uprisings demonstrate a kind of antiauthoritarian democratic dimension of global civil society that has swept the world in an era where national authority has been weakened by the forces of globalization. These protests are a congeries of movements with many different targets and concerns, yet the pattern of citizen rebellion has been clearly established. It surfaces at public protests in central squares, but the underlying current is conveyed through the decentralized, openly accessed global electronic media. These are protests propelled not by terrorist cells but rather by Twitter, Facebook, and YouTube; in fact, Iran's 2009 protest movement has been called the Twitter Revolution. And when the protestors step away from their computers and put down their cell phones and gather together to make a statement, they do so en masse, in public squares.

God is in these public squares as well. In almost every case, religion has played a role. In some cases, it was part of the problem. In Turkey and Iran, the protesters were motivated, in part, by antagonism against government policies that they felt forced religious standards on personal behavior. In other cases, religion was part of the protests themselves, including Christian and Jewish clergy participation in the Occupy Movement, Russian and Ukrainian Orthodox clergy facing each other in the conflicts of Kiev's Independence Square, and moderate Muslim and Coptic Christian support for the protests in Tahrir Square. A mosque adjoining Tahrir became an impromptu medical clinic, and Muslim clergy urged their congregations to join the protests after Friday prayers. In the global era, the citizen-based political protests of civil society are laced with elements of religion. God is in these public squares.

In this book, we have reported on a series of discussions and consultations held all over the world to assess the role that religion is playing in the global era. Our first chapter looked at the way traditional understandings of identity, accountability, and security have been challenged by forces of globalization. Old political and religious institutions have seen their authority tested on numerous fronts as the ways we belong to a community have changed. Increased mobility, improved communication technologies, and the weakening boundaries of the nation-state have spread communities beyond their original boundaries. Such turmoil has resulted in a surge of antiauthoritarianism and a great number of diverse perspectives finding traction in society. A loss of the traditional bases of identity, constantly shifting centers of authority, and a general desire for security in the face of these changes characterize the twenty-first century, and a cacophony of voices have clamored for new ways to anchor us in a global world. This discord of the public is literally heard in Taksim, Zuccotti, and Tahrir, in the public places where revolutionaries gather in hopes of inaugurating a new world order. The global era is an epoch signified by the public square.

Chapter 2 looked at the ways religion has been affected by these shifts. In a volatile period in which boundaries are constantly being challenged, religion provides a stable foundation of identity and a way of being that has its basis in a sacred past. But these religions are not confined to the past, and new religious expressions are continually appearing that both are appropriate for today's world and remain in contact with their spiritual lineage. Many are nontraditional and egalitarian. The megachurches in Texas and Seoul are examples of this new kind of religion, as are the televangelists who garner huge audiences in the Middle East. These new forms are often peaceful, but at times come into violent conflict with other modern poles of identity, especially when they are linked with strident nationalist movements. They clash with the political status quo, as well as with traditional religious authorities, who often see them as challenges to their own influence. Religion is not going away, but it is often taking on powerful new shapes.

In the turbulent waters of the global era, religion can provide solid ground and protection from these new currents, but it can also inspire creative ways to aid the transition into a multicultural world. This is what concerned us in chapter 3, and it led to a deeper understanding of the way religion has reinvented itself into something suitable for the twenty-first century. We saw certain groups—like the Catholic Church in Latin America or the Muslim Brotherhood in the Middle East—challenged by the values of multicultural societies and responding by asserting their traditional identities. At the same time, immigrants often latch onto a traditional religious identity not to reject diversity, but to find a way of fitting into a multicultural society. They find that religion can be linked with ethnicity or fused with a nationalist identity, or it can provide a separate locus of selfhood altogether, a flexibility that is particularly useful in the modern era. The either/or of identity that often leads to violent conflict is both reaffirmed and overcome by the faiths of today, and increasingly we see the emergence of spiritual values common to a number of faiths, providing a common ground for engagement between disparate groups. Religion continues to adapt to its circumstances and is recreating itself for survival in the global community.

Chapter 4 explored some of these possibilities of religious creativity in a global era. It looked at the emergence of a global civil religion that both builds on and is different from the civil religions of the past. Here we turned to Robert Bellah for insight into how this is possible and how the shared values of a global culture are related to the notion of a global civil religion. These common values inspire a great deal of humanitarian activity by nongovernmental organizations and are at the forefront of an emergent culture in which all people are seen as part of a common family. Though these transnational humanitarian efforts can be seen as extensions of particular values, they may also be perceived as harbingers of universal ones. This new ethic of common concern provides the moral commitments that relate to a sense of spiritual unity that provide the global ethic and the global religion of an emerging global civil society.

But such global thinking has its limitations, and these challenges occupied our attention in chapter 5. This chapter explored the question of whether common values are possible when there is seldom consensus on any ethical issue and when our perception of commonality can, in some cases, simply be a projection of our own worldviews. Even values that seem universal, like human rights or the freedom of religious expression, become much more complicated in some cultural contexts and when political power and issues of identity are involved. This fact appears as a significant challenge to the kind of moral complementarity that is also developing in a globalized world. Moral relativity is not a sufficient base for a global civil religion, but neither is the imposition of one group's cultural principles on others. The history of colonialism has left scars across the planet, and these scars are still raw enough that even humanitarian organizations are suspected of being agents of foreign influence. Yet there are threads of commonality woven into the tapestry of the world's cultures, providing the hints that a global civil religion may be emerging after all.

Interestingly, this kind of religion may have been foreseen in the world of ancient Greeks, and it was on display in a public square. In the New Testament section of the Christian Bible, the apostle Paul describes a visit to Athens in which he entered the central square (Acts 17:23). There he encountered a host of temples erected in honor of the various gods in the Greek pantheon. But one temple was remarkable in its absence of a god, at least one with which the populace was familiar. It was inscribed to "the Unknown God." Scholars have speculated that this indicated that the Greeks were aware of other cultures and the possibility of other gods that their tradition had not yet discovered and wanted to be able to revere these gods as well. In the Christian Bible's account, the apostle Paul quickly connected this nameless god's temple to Christianity. Paul delivered a sermon on the spot proclaiming that the Unknown God had, in fact, been revealed, and was the God manifested in Jesus Christ. The Greeks were probably not convinced and continued to keep the temple free of any affiliation so that it could stand as a monument for a religiosity not yet revealed. The incident showed, however, that some two thousand years ago, the idea existed that there was a nameless religiosity that was linked with the unknown religion of a multicultural world.

There still may be an unnamed, unknown religion in the multicultural milieu of global civil society. The God that rises in the tumult of today's global square may be a nameless deity, a symbol of a sense of ultimate meaning, of an unidentified spirituality that knits humanity together in a common spiritual and moral bond. It is not an easy time for adherents of traditional faiths, and it is not an easy time for anyone in the tempest of global changes and the erosion of old nationalist and cultural borders. But this erosion also allows for a freedom from the past and an openness to new forms of sharing, learning, doing, and being in a borderless world. In the Ukraine, after the revolutionary changes that were fostered in the central square of Kiev led to the downfall of the old regime and a rocky new political future, a large contingent of protestors refused to leave. They stayed in the square. For them, this space was not just the symbol of a transition but also of a new society; they wanted to stay there, to wait to see when and in what way it would blossom into life. In the global square, we may all stay encamped, waiting for the promise of a different kind of world, for some time to come.

NOTES

INTRODUCTION

1. Xu Yihua, *Shanghai Transcript,* lines 203–5. This transcript, and all other transcripts mentioned in these notes, are accessible on line at the project's website at http://www.global.ucsb.edu/luceproject/general/index.html.

2. Peter Berger, "Religion and Global Civil Society," in *Religion in Global Civil Society,* ed. Mark Juergensmeyer (New York: Oxford University Press, 2005), 11–22.

3. Jacob Olupona, *Africa and the Middle East Transcript,* lines 693–95.

4. Lamia Karim, *South and Southeast Asia Transcript,* lines 2111–15.

5. Manindra Thakur, *Delhi Transcript,* lines 2336–42.

6. For the relation between religion and secularism, see Craig Calhoun, Mark Juergensmeyer, and Jonathan VanAntwerpen, eds., *Rethinking Secularism* (Oxford: Oxford University Press, 2011); Charles Taylor, *A Secular Age* (Cambridge, MA: Belknap Press at Harvard University, 2007); and Talal Asad, *Formations of the Secular: Christianity, Islam, Modernity* (Stanford, CA: Stanford University Press, 2003).

7. Rounaq Jahan, *Delhi Transcript,* lines 1994–99.

8. Ravi Bhatia, *Delhi Transcript,* lines 516–21, video: http://vimeo.com /38951390.

9. Mark Juergensmeyer, *Global Rebellion: Religious Challenges to the Secular State, from Christian Militias to al Qaeda* (Berkeley: University of California Press, 2008).

10. Wilfred Cantwell Smith, *The Meaning and End of Religion* (New York: Macmillan, 1963).

11. William James, *The Varieties of Religious Experience* (New York: Penguin Books, 1982), 31.

12. Francis Fukuyama, *The End of History and the Last Man* (New York: Free Press, 1992).

1. THE SOCIAL TURMOIL OF THE TWENTY-FIRST CENTURY

1. Thomas Friedman, *The Lexus and the Olive Tree* (New York: Farrar, Straus, Giroux, 1999).

2. Surichai Wun'gaeo, *South and Southeast Asia Transcript,* lines 2739–63.

3. Karl Deutsch, *Nationalism and Social Communication* (New York: J. Wiley, 1953).

4. J. P. S. Uberoi, *Delhi Transcript,* lines 1339–73.

5. The debate between Gandhi and Sarvarkar directly preceded the writing of Gandhi's book, *Hind Swaraj, or Indian Home Rule* (Ahmedabad: Navajivan Publishing House, 1944), which was undoubtedly influenced by the debate. See Mark Juergensmeyer's discussion of the incident in "Gandhi vs. Terrorism," in *Daedalus* 136, no. 1 (Winter 2007): 30–39.

6. Bruce Desmond Graham, *Hindu Nationalism and Indian Politics: The Origins and Development of the Bharatiya Jana Sangh* (Cambridge: Cambridge University Press, 2007).

7. I. A. Rehman, *Delhi Transcript,* lines 1923–26.

8. Ibid., lines 1922–23.

9. Amr Abdulrahman, *Cairo Transcript,* lines 862–63.

10. Mark Woodward, *South and Southeast Asia Transcript,* lines 797–98.

11. Robert Dowd, *Africa and the Middle East Transcript,* lines 1740–42, video: http://vimeo.com/38290019.

12. Susanne Hoeber Rudolph, "Introduction: Religion, States and Transnational Civil Society," in *Transnational Religion and Fading States* (Boulder, CO: Westview Press, 1997), 3.

13. Mary Becker, *Latin America and the Caribbean Transcript,* lines 1441–57. Also see Otto Maduro, *Latin America and the Caribbean Transcript,* lines 1522–34.

14. Saad Eddin Ibrahim, *Cairo Transcript,* lines 1378–414. Also see Ashraf El Sharif, *Cairo Transcript,* lines 1150–81.

15. Fukuyama, *The End of History and the Last Man.*

16. See also Mark Juergensmeyer, *Terror in the Mind of God: The Global Rise of Religious Violence* (Berkeley: University of California Press, 2003).

17. For more on the concept of the field, see Pierre Bourdieu, *Outline of a Theory of Practice* (New York: Cambridge University Press, 1977).

2. RELIGION TUMBLES AND TURNS

1. Robert Bellah, "Civil Religion in America," *Daedalus* 96, no. 1 (Winter 1967): 1–21. On the changing American religious landscape, see Wade Clark Roof, *American Mainline Religion: Its Changing Shape and Future* (New Brunswick, NJ: Rutgers University Press, 1987), and on growing secularism in America, see David Niose,

Nonbeliever Nation: The Rise of Secular Americans (New York: Palgrave Macmillan, 2012).

2. John Chathanatt, *Delhi Transcript,* line 2255.

3. These accusations came from the embassy of the People's Republic of China to the United States, "Falun Gong Followers Cruel in Killing the Innocent," July 14, 2003, www.china-embassy.org/eng/zt/ppflg/t36618.htm.

4. For his poetry where he references "the day of reckoning draws near," see Li Hongzhi, "The Red Tide's Wane" at the Falun Dafa's official website: http://en .minghui.org/html/articles/2005/10/19/66050.html.

5. "Mujaddidun (Amr Khaled Reality TV show) on CNN," YouTube video, 2:24, posted by "Ethar El-Katatney," April 27, 2010, www.youtube.com /watch?v=S7XWkGqmo34.

6. I. A. Rehman, *Delhi Transcript,* lines 1069–73, video following statement: http://vimeo.com/20225154.

7. See the official Ahmadiyya website, www.alislam.org/introduction/index .html.

8. Shrivatsa Goswami, *Delhi Transcript,* lines 598–605.

9. Ibid., lines 1624–31.

10. Pralay Kanungo, *Delhi Transcript,* lines 1653–57, video: http://vimeo .com/38951393.

11. Eve Darian-Smith, *Religion, Race, Rights: Landmarks in the History of Modern Anglo-American Law* (Portland, OR: Hart Publications, 2010).

12. Carlos Escude, *Buenos Aires Transcript,* lines 878–79.

13. Leonor Slavsky, *Buenos Aires Transcript,* lines 106–8.

14. Leonor Slavsky, *Buenos Aires Transcript,* lines 464–66.

15. *Holy Bible,* New Revised Standard Version, Matthew 5:3, Luke 6:20.

16. Marianne Loewe, *Latin America and the Caribbean Transcript,* lines 166–70, video: http://vimeo.com/10422766.

17. Cecelia Lynch, *Latin America and the Caribbean Transcript, lines* 644–49, video: http://vimeo.com/11703769.

18. Ibid.

19. Mohammed Bamyeh, *Africa and the Middle East Transcript,* lines 514–77, video: http://vimeo.com/38289930.

20. Ibid.

21. Jeffrey Haynes, *Africa and the Middle East Transcript,* lines 1009–22. See also Mohammed Bamyeh, *Africa and the Middle East Transcript,* lines 780–98, and Mae Cannon, *Africa and the Middle East Transcript,* lines 736–40.

22. See Calhoun, Juergensmeyer, and VanAntwerpen, eds., *Rethinking Secularism,* for essays exploring this issue.

23. Mohammed Bamyeh, *Africa and the Middle East Transcript,* lines 808–22.

24. Ibid.

25. See Ikhwan Web: The Muslim Brotherhood's official English website, http:// www.ikhwanweb.com/article.php?id=31670.

1. Pat Robertson, quoted in Meredith Bennett-Smith, "Pat Robertson Claims Islam Is 'Demonic' and 'Not a Religion' but an Economic System," *The Huffington Post,* February 13, 2013, www.huffingtonpost.com/2013/02/13/pat-robertson-claims-islam-demonic-not-a-religion_n_2680895.html.

2. Benedict Anderson, *Imagined Communities: Reflections on the Origin and Spread of Nationalism* (New York: Verso, 2006 [1983]).

3. Mohammed Bamyeh, *Africa and the Middle East Transcript,* lines 529–32, video: http://vimeo.com/38289930.

4. Samah Khalil Faried, *Cairo Transcript,* lines 805–8.

5. Amr Abdulrahman, *Cairo Transcript,* lines 814–24, video: http://vimeo.com/32226438

6. Siti Syamsiyatun, *Shanghai Transcript,* lines 1965–87.

7. Ibid, lines 1903–17.

8. A. N. Burhani, "Lakum dinukum wa-liya dini: The Muhammadiyah's Stance towards Interfaith Relations," *Islam and Christian-Muslim Relations* 22, no. 3 (July 2011): 330.

9. Holy Qur'an, 5:48.

10. Holy Qur'an, 109:6.

11. Mark Woodward, *South and Southeast Asia Transcript,* lines 803–7.

12. Muhamad Ali, *South and Southeast Asia Transcript,* lines 888–94.

13. Mary Zurbuchen, *South and Southeast Asia Transcript,* lines 1205–14.

14. Virginia Garrard-Burnett, *Latin America and the Caribbean Transcript,* lines 104–18.

15. Ibid.

16. Ibid, lines 104–9.

17. Kurt Frieder, *Latin America and the Caribbean Transcript,* lines 611–20, video: http://vimeo.com/10425230.

18. Abdullahi Ahmed an-Na'im, *Islam and the Secular State: Negotiating the Future of Shari'a* (Cambridge, MA: Harvard University Press, 2008).

19. Robert Dowd, *Africa and the Middle East Transcript,* lines 738–43, video: http://vimeo.com/38290019.

20. Jacob Olupona, *Africa and the Middle East Transcript,* lines 676–77.

21. Benedict Anderson, interview by Lorenz Khazaleh, translated by Matthew Whiting, at the University of Oslo, http://www.uio.no/english/research/interfaculty-research-areas/culcom/news/2005/anderson.html.

22. Surichai Wun'gaeo, *South and Southeast Asia Transcript,* lines 2751–55.

23. James Wellman, *Latin America and the Caribbean Transcript,* lines 401–6.

24. Pierre Bourdieu and Loïc J. D. Wacquant, *An Invitation to Reflexive Sociology* (Chicago: University of Chicago Press, 1992), 119.

25. Tadaatsu Tajima, *Shanghai Transcript,* lines 412–16.

26. Kai Sheng, *Shanghai Transcript,* lines 1405–17.

27. Ibid.

28. Somboon Chungprampree, *Shanghai Transcript,* lines 1314–91.

29. Ranjana Mukhopadhyaya, *Delhi Transcript,* lines 1809–26.

30. Rosalind Hackett, *Africa and the Middle East Transcript,* lines 584–90, video: http://vimeo.com/38290020.

31. Surichai Wun'gaeo, *South and Southeast Asia Transcript,* lines 1750–58.

32. T. N. Madan, *Cairo Transcript,* lines 908–22.

33. Dominador Bombongan, *Shanghai Transcript,* lines 1661–68.

34. Mohammed Bamyeh, *Africa and the Middle East Transcript,* lines 566–76, video: http://vimeo.com/38289930.

35. Jeffrey Haynes, *Africa and the Middle East Transcript,* lines 3193–203.

36. Jennifer Hughes, *Latin America and the Caribbean Transcript,* lines 31–41, video: http://vimeo.com/10424881.

37. Virginia Garrard-Burnett, *Latin America and the Caribbean Transcript,* lines 271–77.

38. Ibid.

39. Robert Dowd, *Africa and the Middle East Transcript,* lines 3211–14.

40. Ibid.

41. Elizabeth Collins, *South and Southeast Asia Transcript,* lines 2925–31.

4. COSMOPOLITAN RELIGION AT WORK

1. Robert Bellah, *Religion in Human Evolution: From the Paleolithic to the Axial Age* (Cambridge, MA: Belknap Press of Harvard University Press, 2011), video at http://vimeo.com/40404248, https://vimeo.com/40404242, and https://vimeo.com/40404236.

2. Bellah, "Civil Religion in America" (*Daedalus* 96:1 Winter 1967, 1–21). This essay has been most recently reprinted in *The Robert Bellah Reader,* ed. Robert N. Bellah and Steven M. Tipton (Durham, NC: Duke University Press, 2006), 225–45.

3. Jean-Jacques Rousseau, *The Social Contract* (New York: Dutton, 1950 [1762]), especially book 4, chapter 8.

4. Émile Durkheim, *Elementary Forms of Religious Life,* trans. Karen E. Fields (New York: Free Press, 1995 [1912]).

5. Video of Bellah reading his unpublished paper, "Is Global Civil Society Possible?" is available online (in three parts): http://vimeo.com/40404248, https://vimeo.com/40404242, and https://vimeo.com/40404236.

6. See Mark Juergensmeyer, "How Robert Bellah (1927–2013) Changed the Study of Religion," *Religion Dispatches,* August 5, 2013, http://religiondispatches .org/how-robert-bellah-1927-2013-changed-the-study-of-religion; and Mark Juergensmeyer, "In Memoriam: Robert Neelly Bellah (1927–2013)," *Journal of the American Academy of Religion* 81, no. 4 (December 2013): 897–902.

7. Robert Bellah, "Epilogue. Meaning and Modernity: America and the World," in *Meaning and Modernity: Religion, Polity, and Self,* ed. Richard Madsen, William

M. Sullivan, Ann Swidler, Steven M. Tipton, and Robert N. Bellah (Berkeley: University of California Press, 2001), 255–76.

8. Smith, *Towards a World Theology,* 11–14.

9. See the video of Bellah reading his unpublished paper cited above.

10. Jürgen Habermas, *The Structural Transformation of the Public Sphere: An Inquiry into a Category of Bourgeois Society* (Cambridge, MA: MIT Press, 1989).

11. See William James, "Moral Equivalent of War," in *The Best American Essays of the Century,* ed. Joyce Carol Oates (Boston: Houghton Mifflin, 2000).

12. Francis (Pope), "Evangelii Gaudium," Roman Catholic Church, November 24, 2013. http://w2.vatican.va/content/francesco/en/apost_exhortations/documents/papa-francesco_esortazione-ap_20131124_evangelii-gaudium.html.

13. Kwame Anthony Appiah, *Cosmopolitanism: Ethics in a World of Strangers* (New York: W.W. Norton, 2006).

14. Ulrich Beck, *The Cosmopolitan Vision,* trans. Ciarian Cronin (Malden, MA: Polity, 2006); and Giles Gunn, *Ideas to Die For: The Cosmopolitan Challenge* (New York: Routledge, 2013).

15. Richard Falk, *On Humane Governance: Toward a New Global Politics* (University Park: Pennsylvania State University Press, 1995).

16. Richard Falk, *Delhi Transcript,* lines 1293–301, video: http://vimeo.com/20317151.

17. Richard Falk, *(Re)Imagining a Humane Global Governance* (New York: Routledge Press, 2014).

18. Mark Juergensmeyer, ed., *Religion in Global Civil Society* (New York: Oxford University Press, 2005).

19. Berger, "Religion and Global Civil Society"; and Susanne Hoeber Rudolph, "Religious Transnationalism," in *Religion in Global Civil Society,* ed. Mark Juergensmeyer (New York: Oxford University Press, 2005), 189–200.

20. Bernard Adeney, *Shanghai Transcript,* lines 1813–20.

21. James Wellman, *Latin America and the Caribbean Transcript,* lines 1753–57, video: http://vimeo.com/11717449.

22. Idris Tsechoev, *Moscow Transcript,* lines 777–83.

23. David Palmer, *Shanghai Transcript,* lines 488–96.

24. Mark Woodward, *South and Southeast Asia Transcript,* lines 628–33.

25. Thomas Tighe, *Latin America and the Caribbean Transcript,* lines 1170–73, video: http://vimeo.com/11698833.

26. Katherine Marshall, *South and Southeast Asia Transcript,* lines 544–53.

27. Ria Shibata, *South and Southeast Asia Transcript,* lines 451–73.

28. For information on the role of Buddhist monks and the HIV/AIDS problem in Cambodia, see UNICEF's official website: http://www.unicef.org/aids/cambodia_39935.html.

29. Katherine Marshall, *South and Southeast Asia Transcript,* lines 843–54.

30. Ibid., lines 852–54.

31. Mary Becker, *Latin America and the Caribbean Transcript,* lines 1020–26 and 1384–98, video: http://vimeo.com/11698364.

32. For more information on Fonkoze USA and Father Joseph Philippe, see Fonkoze's official website: http://fonkoze.org/about-fonkoze/story.

33. Anindita Chakrabarti, *Delhi Transcript,* lines 410–42.

34. Pralay Kanungo, *Delhi Transcript,* lines 1645–48, video: http://vimeo.com/38951393.

35. Victoria Riskin, *Latin America and the Caribbean Transcript,* lines 1152–58, video: http://vimeo.com/11700218.

36. Rowena Robinson, *Delhi Transcript,* lines 1207–10, video: http://vimeo.com/20274637.

37. Ibid.

38. John Chathanatt, *Delhi Transcript,* lines 1251–61, video: http://vimeo.com/20316927.

39. Ibid.

40. Catherine Bell, *Ritual Theory, Ritual Practice* (New York: Oxford University Press, 1992), 185.

41. See Mark Juergensmeyer, "2009 Presidential Address: Beyond Words and War: The Global Future of Religion," *Journal of the American Academy of Religion* 78, no. 4 (December 2010): 882–95.

42. See, for example, Calhoun, Juergensmeyer, and VanAntwerpen, eds., *Rethinking Secularism.*

43. Talal Asad, *Geneologies of Religion: Discipline and Reasons of Power in Christianity and Islam* (Baltimore, MD: Johns Hopkins Press, 1993), esp. chap. 1.

44. I. A. Rehman, *Delhi Transcript,* lines 2010–13.

45. Thomas Tighe, *Latin America and the Caribbean Transcript,* lines 1190–94, video: http://vimeo.com/11698833.

46. Ibid., lines 1224–34, video: http://vimeo.com/11698833.

5. THE ANNOYING CERTAINTY OF GLOBAL VIEWS

1. Sarah Eskow, *Africa and the Middle East Transcript,* lines 2252–58, 2277–81.

2. Waleed Al Ansary, *Africa and the Middle East Transcript,* lines 2345–50. See also Jacop Olupona's comments at *Africa and the Middle East Transcript,* lines 2901–41.

3. Steve Eskow, *Africa and the Middle East Transcript,* lines 2539–85.

4. Waleed Al Ansary, *Africa and the Middle East Transcript,* lines 3030–54.

5. Mohammed Bamyeh, *Africa and the Middle East Transcript,* lines 2728 and 2731.

6. Father Mikhail Zakharov, *Moscow Transcript,* lines 1812–24; video: http://vimeo.com/127954713.

7. Mikhail I. Gelvanovsky, *Moscow Transcript,* lines 1637–58; video: http://vimeo.com/127954713.

8. The history between Tibet and China is admittedly more complicated than that of Hawaii and the United States. For a good discussion, see John Powers, *History as Propaganda: Tibetan Exiles versus the People's Republic of China* (New York: Oxford University Press, 2014).

9. Mikhail I. Gelvanovsky, *Moscow Transcript,* lines 1697–720.

10. Mae Cannon, *Africa and the Middle East Transcript,* lines 1463–69

11. Lamia Karim, *South and Southeast Asia Transcript,* lines 1593–99.

12. Ranjana Mukhopadhyaya, *Delhi Transcript,* lines 1311–17, video: http://vimeo.com/20318320.

13. Samah Khalil Faried, *Cairo Transcript,* lines 805–8.

14. Amr Abdulrahman, *Cairo Transcript,* lines 810–41, video: http://vimeo.com/32226438.

15. Katherine Marshall, *South and Southeast Asia Transcript,* lines 814–32.

16. Richard Falk, *Delhi Transcript,* lines 1835–50.

17. For a good discussion of China's participation in UN Human Rights, see Ann Kent, *China, the United Nations, and Human Rights: The Limits of Compliance* (Philadelphia: University of Pennsylvania Press, 1999).

18. Quoted in Abdulaziz M. Alwasil, "Saudi Arabia's Engagement in, and Interaction with, the UN Human Rights System: An Analytical Review" *International Journal of Human Rights* 14, no. 7 (December 2010): 1075.

19. Ibid.

20. Carlos Escude, *Buenos Aires Transcript,* lines 626–34.

21. Frederick (Fritz) Lampe, *Africa and the Middle East Transcript,* lines 1875–78.

22. A good examination of the way religion, law, and ideas of race combined in the early American expansion can be found in Darian-Smith, *Religion, Race, Rights,* chap. 6.

23. See Geoffrey A. Fowler, "China Opens Doors to Quake Relief, but Not Missionaries" *Wall Street Journal,* May 31, 2008.

24. Katherine Marshall, *South and Southeast Asia Transcript,* lines 1323–25.

25. Elizabeth Collins, *South and Southeast Asia Transcript,* lines 945–52, video: http://vimeo.com/38288050.

26. Fernando Lopez-Alves, *Latin America and the Caribbean Transcript,* lines 1574–84.

27. Mary Zurbuchen, *South and Southeast Asia Transcript,* lines 1205–14.

28. Mark Woodward, *South and Southeast Asia Transcript,* lines 657–67, video: http://vimeo.com/38288176.

29. For more information on UNAMI, see their official website: www.uniraq.org/index.php?lang=en.

30. Reported in "The Insurgency," *PBS Frontline,* www.pbs.org/wgbh/pages/frontline/insurgency/etc/script.html.

31. Richard Falk, *Africa and the Middle East Transcript,* lines 1990–96.

32. Ibid.

33. Caroline Meyer-White, *South and Southeast Asia Transcript,* lines 1121–35, video: http://vimeo.com/38288049.

34. Ibid.

35. Mae Cannon, *Africa and the Middle East Transcript,* lines 1148–55 and 2169–78, video: http://vimeo.com/38289929.

36. Dwight Hopkins, *Africa and the Middle East Transcript,* lines 1299–302, video: http://vimeo.com/38289855.

CONCLUSION

1. Clifford Geertz, "Centers, Kings, and Charisma: Reflections on the Symbolics of Power," in *Culture and Its Creators: Essays in Honor of Edmund Shils,* ed. Joseph Ben-David and Terry Nichols Clark (Chicago: University of Chicago Press, 1977); reprinted in Clifford Geertz, *Local Knowledge: Further Essays in Interpretive Anthropology* (New York: Basic Books, 1983), 121–46, 151.

BIBLIOGRAPHY

Al-Islam. "An Overview." Ahmadiyya Muslim Community. www.alislam.org /introduction/index.html.

Alwasil, Abdulaziz M. "Saudi Arabia's Engagement in, and Interaction with, the UN Human Rights System: An Analytical Review." *The International Journal of Human Rights* 14, no. 7 (December 2010): 1072–91.

Anderson, Benedict. *Imagined Communities: Reflections on the Origin and Spread of Nationalism.* New York: Verso, 2006 [1983].

———. Interview by Lorenz Khazaleh, translated by Matthew Whiting. University of Oslo. www.uio.no/english/research/interfaculty-research-areas/culcom /news/2005/anderson.html.

An-Na'im, Abdullahi Ahmed. *Islam and the Secular State: Negotiating the Future of Shari'a.* Cambridge, MA: Harvard University Press, 2008.

Appiah, Kwame Anthony. *Cosmopolitanism: Ethics in a World of Strangers.* New York: W. W. Norton, 2006.

Asad, Talal. *Formations of the Secular: Christianity, Islam, Modernity.* Stanford, CA: Stanford University Press, 2003.

———. *Genealogies of Religion: Discipline and Reasons of Power in Christianity and Islam.* Baltimore, MD: Johns Hopkins Press, 1993.

Beck, Ulrich. *The Cosmopolitan Vision.* Translated by Ciarian Cronin. Malden, MA: Polity, 2006.

Bell, Catherine. *Ritual Theory, Ritual Practice.* New York: Oxford University Press, 1992.

Bellah, Robert. "Civil Religion in America." *Daedalus* 96, no. 1 (Winter 1967): 1–21.

———. "Epilogue. Meaning and Modernity: America and the World." In *Meaning and Modernity: Religion, Polity and Self,* edited by Richard Madsen, William M. Sullivan, Ann Swidler, Steven M. Tipton, and Robert N. Bellah. Berkeley: University of California Press, 2001, 255–76.

———. *Religion in Human Evolution: From the Paleolithic to the Axial Age.* Cambridge, MA: Belknap Press of Harvard University Press, 2011.

Bennett-Smith, Meredith. "Pat Robertson Claims Islam is 'Demonic' and 'Not a Religion' but an Economic System." *The Huffington Post,* February 13, 2013, www.huffingtonpost.com/2013/02/13/pat-robertson-claims-islam-demonic-not-a-religion_n_2680895.html.

Berger, Peter. "Religion and Global Civil Society." In *Religion in Global Civil Society,* edited by Mark Juergensmeyer, 11–22. New York: Oxford University Press, 2005.

Bourdieu, Pierre. *Outline of a Theory of Practice.* New York: Cambridge University Press, 1977.

Bourdieu, Pierre, and Loïc J. D. Wacquant. *An Invitation to Reflexive Sociology.* Chicago: University of Chicago Press, 1992.

Burhani, A. N. "Lakum dinukum wa-liya dini: The Muhammadiyah's Stance towards Interfaith Relations." *Islam and Christian-Muslim Relations* 22, no. 3 (July 2011): 329–42.

Calhoun, Craig, Mark Juergensmeyer, and Jonathan VanAntwerpen, eds. *Rethinking Secularism.* Oxford: Oxford University Press, 2011.

Darian-Smith, Eve. *Religion, Race, Rights: Landmarks in the History of Modern Anglo-American Law.* Portland, OR: Hart Publications, 2010.

Deutsch, Karl. *Nationalism and Social Communication.* New York: J. Wiley, 1953.

Durkheim, Émile. *Elementary Forms of Religious Life.* Translated by Karen E. Fields. New York: Free Press, 1995 [1912].

Falk, Richard. *On Humane Governance: Toward a New Global Politics.* University Park, PA: Pennsylvania State University Press, 1995.

———. *(Re)Imagining a Humane Global Governance.* New York: Routledge Press, 2014.

Fowler, Geoffrey A. "China Opens Doors to Quake Relief, but Not Missionaries." *Wall Street Journal,* May 31, 2008.

Francis (pope). "Evangelii Gaudium." Roman Catholic Church, November 24, 2013. http://w2.vatican.va/content/francesco/en/apost_exhortations/documents/papa-francesco_esortazione-ap_20131124_evangelii-gaudium.html.

Friedman, Thomas. *The Lexus and the Olive Tree.* New York: Farrar, Straus, Giroux, 1999.

Fukuyama, Francis. *The End of History and the Last Man.* New York: Free Press, 1992.

Gandhi, Mohandas. *Hind Swaraj, or Indian Home Rule.* Ahmedabad, India: Navajivan Publishing House, 1944.

Geertz, Clifford. "Centers, Kings, and Charisma: Reflections on the Symbolics of Power." In *Local Knowledge: Further Essays in Interpretive Anthropology.* New York: Basic Books, 1983.

Graham, Bruce Desmond. *Hindu Nationalism and Indian Politics: The Origins and Development of the Bharatiya Jana Sangh.* Cambridge: Cambridge University Press, 2007.

Gunn, Giles. *Ideas to Die For: The Cosmopolitan Challenge.* New York: Routledge, 2013.

Habermas, Jürgen. *The Structural Transformation of the Public Sphere: An Inquiry into a Category of Bourgeois Society.* Cambridge, MA: MIT Press, 1989.

Hongzhi, Li. "The Red Tide's Wane." Falun Dafa. http://en.minghui.org/html /articles/2005/10/19/66050.html.

James, William. "Moral Equivalent of War." In *The Best American Essays of the Century,* edited by Joyce Carol Oates. Boston: Houghton Mifflin, 2000.

———. *The Varieties of Religious Experience.* New York: Penguin Books, 1982.

Juergensmeyer, Mark. "2009 Presidential Address: Beyond Words and War: The Global Future of Religion." *Journal of the American Academy of Religion* 78, no. 4 (December 2010): 882–95.

———. "Gandhi vs. Terrorism." *Daedalus* 136, no. 1 (Winter 2007): 30–39.

———. *Global Rebellion: Religious Challenges to the Secular State, from Christian Militias to al Qaeda.* Berkeley: University of California Press, 2008.

———. "How Robert Bellah (1927–2013) Changed the Study of Religion." *Religion Dispatches,* August 5, 2013, http://religiondispatches.org/how-robert-bellah-1927– 2013-changed-the-study-of-religion.

———. "In Memoriam: Robert Neely Bellah (1927–2013). *Journal of the American Academy of Religion* 81, no. 4 (December 2013): 897–902.

———, ed. *Religion in Global Civil Society.* New York: Oxford University Press, 2005.

———. *Terror in the Mind of God: The Global Rise of Religious Violence.* Berkeley: University of California Press, 2003.

Kent, Ann. *China, the United Nations, and Human Rights: The Limits of Compliance.* Philadelphia: University of Pennsylvania Press, 1999.

Muslim Brotherhood. "Muslim Brotherhood Leader Heshmat: Revolution Continues Until Coup Defeat." *Ikhwan Web.* www.ikhwanweb.com/article.php?id= 31670.

Niose, David. *Nonbeliever Nation: The Rise of Secular Americans.* New York: Palgrave Macmillan, 2012.

People's Republic of China. "Falun Gong Followers Cruel in Killing Innocent." Embassy of the People's Republic of China to the United States, July 14, 2003, www.china-embassy.org/eng/zt/ppflg/t36618.htm.

Powers, John. *History as Propaganda: Tibetan Exiles versus the People's Republic of China.* New York: Oxford University Press, 2004.

Roof, Wade Clark. *American Mainline Religion: Its Changing Shape and Future.* New Brunswick, NJ: Rutgers University Press, 1987.

Rousseau, Jean-Jacques. *The Social Contract.* New York: Dutton, 1950.

Rudolph, Susanne Hoeber. "Introduction: Religion, States and Transnational Civil Society." In *Transnational Religion and Fading States.* Boulder, CO: Westview Press, 1997.

———. "Religious Transnationalism." In *Religion in Global Civil Society,* edited by Mark Juergensmeyer, 189–200. New York: Oxford University Press, 2005.

Smith, Wilfred Cantwell. *The Meaning and End of Religion.* New York: Macmillan, 1963.

———. *Towards a World Theology: Faith and the Comparative History of Religion.* Philadelphia: Westminster Press, 1981.

Taylor, Charles. *A Secular Age.* Cambridge, MA: Belknap Press at Harvard University, 2007.

Tocqueville, Alexis de. *Democracy in America.* London: Oxford University Press 1946 [1835, 1840].

WORKSHOP PARTICIPANTS

All affiliations listed below were current at the time of the workshops.

Amr Abdulrahman
Doctoral Researcher
Essex University
United Kingdom
Cairo 1 Workshop
Cairo 2 Workshop

Bernard Adeney-Risakotta
International Representative
Indonesian Consortium for Religious Studies (ICRS-Yogya), Graduate School
Gadjah Mada University, Yogyakarta, Indonesia
Shanghai Workshop

Muhamad Ali
Assistant Professor of Religious Studies
University of California, Riverside
South and Southeast Asia Workshop

Paul Amar
Associate Professor of Global and International Studies
University of California, Santa Barbara
Cairo 1 Workshop
Cairo 2 Workshop (Co-convenor)
Africa and the Middle East Workshop

Richard P. Appelbaum
Professor of Sociology and Global and International Studies
University of California, Santa Barbara
Planning Workshop
Networking Workshop

R. Scott Appleby
Professor of History
Kroc Institute for International Peace Studies
University of Notre Dame
Planning Workshop

Greg Auberry
Country Representative
Catholic Relief Services, Cambodia
Shanghai Workshop

Mohammed Bamyeh
Professor of Sociology
Editor, International Sociology Review of Books (ISRB)
University of Pittsburgh
Africa and the Middle East Workshop

Mary Becker
Member, National Board
Fonkoze USA
Latin America and the Caribbean Workshop

Robert Bellah
Elliott Professor of Sociology, Emeritus
University of California, Berkeley
Consultant

Ravi Bhatia
Professor of Physics and Education, Emeritus
University of Delhi
Executive Member, International Peace Research Association
Convener, Religion and Peace Commission
Delhi Workshop

Sarah Blackmun-Eskow
President, The Pangaea Network
Africa and the Middle East Workshop

Zoya S. Bocharova
Professor, Faculty of Global Processes
Lomonosov Moscow State University
Moscow Workshop

Dominador Bombongan
Dean, College of Liberal Arts
De La Salle University, Philippines
Shanghai Workshop

Kathleen Bruhn
Professor of Comparative Politics and Latin American Studies
University of California, Santa Barbara
Latin America and the Caribbean Workshop

Craig Calhoun
President, Social Science Research Council
Professor of Sociology
New York University
Consultant

Juan Campo
Associate Professor of Religious Studies
University of California, Santa Barbara
South and Southeast Asia Workshop
Cairo 1 Workshop (Co-convenor)
Cairo 2 Workshop
Africa and the Middle East Workshop

Magda Campo
Lecturer in Religious Studies
University of California, Santa Barbara
Cairo 1 Workshop
Cairo 2 Workshop

Mae Elise Cannon
Senior Director of Advocacy and Outreach—Middle East

World Vision United States
Africa and the Middle East Workshop

Mercedes Carluccio
Project Director, Democracia Global
Buenos Aires Workshop

Anindita Chakrabarti
Assistant Professor of Sociology
Indian Institute of Technology, Kanpur
Delhi Workshop

Fr. John Chathanatt
Principal, Vidyajyoti College of Theology
India Social Institute, Delhi, India
Delhi Workshop

Somboon Chungprampree
Executive Secretary, International Network of Engaged Buddhists, Thailand
Shanghai Workshop

Sarah Cline
Professor of Latin American History
University of California, Santa Barbara
Latin America and the Caribbean Workshop

Nadege Clitandre
Assistant Professor of Global and International Studies
University of California, Santa Barbara
Latin America and the Caribbean Workshop
Africa and the Middle East Workshop

Elizabeth Collins
Professor of World Religions and Southeast Asian Studies
Ohio University
South and Southeast Asia Workshop

Brian Cox
Project Director, Kashmir and the Middle East
International Center for Religion and Diplomacy (ICRD)
Planning Workshop

Eve Darian-Smith
Professor of Global and International Studies
University of California, Santa Barbara
South and Southeast Asia Workshop

James Donahue
President, Graduate Theological Union
South and Southeast Asia Workshop
Africa and the Middle East Workshop

Robert Dowd
Assistant Professor of Political Science
University of Notre Dame
Africa and the Middle East Workshop

Waleed El Ansary
University Chair in Islamic Studies
Xavier University, Cincinnati
Africa and the Middle East Workshop

Ahmad El Bendary
Founder, Islamic Relief
Planning Workshop

Osama El Mahdy
Editor, *Al-Masry Al-Youm*
Cairo, Egypt
Cairo 1 Workshop

Ashraf El Sherif
Adjunct Professor of Political Science
American University in Cairo
Cairo 1 Workshop

Hilal Elver
Fellow, Orfalea Center for Global and International Studies
University of California, Santa Barbara
Delhi Workshop
South and Southeast Asia Workshop
Africa and the Middle East Workshop

Fatma Emam
Nazra for Feminist Studies
Cairo, Egypt
Cairo 2 Workshop

Carlos Escude
Director, Centro de Estudios Internacionales y de Educacion para la Globalizacion (CEIEG)
Universidad del Cema (UCEMA)
Buenos Aires Workshop (Co-convenor)

Steve Eskow
Chair, The Pangaea Network
Director, External Affairs, Ghana Telecom University College
Africa and the Middle East Workshop

Rebeca Gonzalez Esteves
Graduate Student, Universidad del Cema (UCEMA)
Buenos Aires Workshop

Richard Falk
Albert G. Milbank Professor of International Law at Princeton University, Emeritus
Fellow, Orfalea Center for Global and International Studies
University of California, Santa Barbara
Planning Workshop
Networking Workshop
Latin America and the Caribbean Workshop
Delhi Workshop
South and Southeast Asia Workshop
Africa and the Middle East Workshop

Samah Khalil Faried
Lecturer in Sociology
Ain Shams University, Cairo
Cairo 1 Workshop

Tao Feiya
Professor of History
Shanghai University
Shanghai Workshop

John Fitzmier
Executive Director, American Academy of Religion
Networking Workshop

Kurt Frieder
Founder and Director, Fundacion Huesped, Argentina
Buenos Aires Workshop
Latin America and the Caribbean Workshop

Nancy Gallagher
Professor of Middle East History
University of California, Santa Barbara
Cairo 1 Workshop
Cairo 2 Workshop

Virginia Garrard-Burnett
Professor of Religious Studies
University of Texas, Austin
Latin America and the Caribbean Workshop

Mark D. Gearan
President, Hobart and William Smith Colleges
Planning Workshop

Mikhail I. Gelvanovsky
Director, Institute for Religious and Social Studies
Russian Academy of Science
Moscow Workshop

Acharya Shrivatsa Goswami
Sri Radharaman Mandir
Vrindavan, India
Delhi Workshop

Laura Grillo
Professor of History of Religions
Pacifica Graduate Institute
Africa and the Middle East Workshop

Giles Gunn
Professor of English and Global and International Studies

University of California, Santa Barbara
Planning Workshop
Networking Workshop
Buenos Aires Workshop
Latin America and the Caribbean Workshop

Changgang Guo
Professor of History, Dean of Graduate Studies
Director of the Center for Global Studies
Shanghai University
Shanghai Workshop (Co-convenor)

Beatriz Gurevich
Special Advisor, Centro de Estudios Internacionales y de Educacion para la Globalizacion (CEIG)
Universidad del Cema (UCEMA)
Buenos Aires Workshop

Rosalind I.J. Hackett
Professor of Religious Studies
University of Tennessee
Africa and the Middle East Workshop

Jeffrey Haynes
Director, Center for the Study of Religion, Conflict, and Cooperation
London Metropolitan University
Africa and the Middle East Workshop

William Headley
Dean, Joan B. Kroc School of Peace Studies
University of San Diego
Planning Workshop
Networking Workshop
South and Southeast Asia Workshop
Africa and The Middle East Workshop

David Hirschmann
Professor, School of International Service
American University
Networking Workshop

Jin Hongwei
Imam and President, Shanghai Islamic Association, China
Shanghai Workshop

She Hongyu
Director, The Amity Foundation
Shanghai Workshop

Dwight Hopkins
Founder, International Association of Black Religions and Spiritualities
Professor, Divinity School
University of Chicago
Africa and the Middle East Workshop

Jennifer Hughes
Associate Professor of Religious Studies
University of California, Riverside
Latin America and the Caribbean Workshop

Barbara Ibrahim
Founding Director, John D. Gerhart Center for Philanthropy and Civic Engagement
Cairo, Egypt
Cairo 1 Workshop

Ishak Ibrahim
Researcher, Egyptian Initiative for Personal Rights
Cairo, Egypt
Cairo 1 Workshop

Saad Ibrahim
Founder, Ibn Khaldun Center for Development Studies
Cairo, Egypt
Planning Workshop
Cairo 1 Workshop

Ilya Ilyin
Dean, Faculty of Global Processes
Lomonosov Moscow State University
Moscow Workshop (Co-convenor)

Rounaq Jahan
Distinguished Fellow, Centre for Policy Dialogue
Dhaka, Bangladesh
and Senior Research Scholar, School of International and Public Affairs
Columbia University
Delhi Workshop

Patrick James
Director, Center for International Studies
University of Southern California
Networking Workshop

Douglas M. Johnston
Founder, International Center for Religion and Diplomacy (ICRD)
Planning Workshop

Mark Juergensmeyer
Professor of Sociology and Global and International Studies
Director, Orfalea Center for Global and International Studies
University of California, Santa Barbara
Convenor, All Workshops

Sheng Kai
Associate Professor of Philosophy
Tsinghua University
Shanghai Workshop

Pralay Kanungo
Professor, Center for Political Studies
Jawaharlal Nehru University, New Delhi, India
Delhi Workshop

Lamia Karim
Associate Professor of Anthropology
University of Oregon
South and Southeast Asia Workshop

Sanjeev Khagram
Associate Professor of Public Affairs and International Studies
Evans School of Public Affairs

University of Washington
Networking Workshop

Heup Young Kim
Professor of Systematic Theology
Kangnam University, Korea
Shanghai Workshop

Sebastian Kobaru
Graduate Student, UCEMA
Buenos Aires Workshop

Frederick (Fritz) J. Lampe
Adjunct Faculty in Anthropology
Northern Arizona University
Africa and the Middle East Workshop

Terril Lautz
Vice President, Henry Luce Foundation
Planning Workshop

Olga G. Leonova
Professor, Faculty of Global Processes
Lomonosov Moscow State University
Moscow Workshop

Ann Lesch
Dean, American University in Cairo
Cairo 2 Workshop

Xiaoping Li
Professor of Sociology
East China Normal University
Shanghai Workshop

Ma Lirong
Associate Director, Middle East Studies Institute,
Shanghai International Studies University
Shanghai Workshop

Yi Liu
Associate Professor of History
Shanghai University
Shanghai Workshop

Marianne Loewe
Executive Director, Concern America
Latin America and the Caribbean Workshop

Fernando Lopez-Alves
Professor of Sociology
University of California, Santa Barbara
Special Advisor, CEIG UCEMA
Buenos Aires Workshop
Latin America and the Caribbean (Co-convenor)

Andy Lower
Executive Director, The Eleos Foundation
Santa Barbara, California
Networking Workshop

Cecelia Lynch
Associate Professor of Political Science and International Studies
Director, Center for Global Peace and Conflict Studies
University of California, Irvine
Planning Workshop
Latin America and the Caribbean Workshop

T. N. Madan
Professor of Sociology, Emeritus
Institute of Economic Growth
Delhi University
Honorary Fellow, Royal Anthropological Institute, London
Delhi Workshop

Otto Maduro
Professor of World Christianity
Drew University
Latin America and the Caribbean Workshop

Katherine Marshall
Senior Fellow, Berkley Center for Religion, Peace, and World Affairs
Executive Director, World Faiths Development Dialogue
Georgetown University
Planning Workshop
Networking Workshop
Latin America and the Caribbean Workshop
Delhi Workshop
South and Southeast Asia Workshop

Aashish Mehta
Assistant Professor of Global and International Studies
University of California, Santa Barbara
South and Southeast Asia Workshop

Barbara Metcalf
Professor of History, Emerita
University of California, Davis
South and Southeast Asia Workshop

Caroline Meyer-White
Project Manager, Engineers without Borders, Pakistan Region
South and Southeast Asia Workshop

Claudine Michel
Professor of Black Studies
University of California, Santa Barbara
Latin America and the Caribbean Workshop

Bidyut Mohanty
Chair, Women's Studies Department
Institute of Social Sciences, New Delhi, India
Fellow, Orfalea Center for Global and International Studies
University of California, Santa Barbara
Delhi Workshop

Manoranjan Mohanty
Distinguished Professor of Political Science
Council for Social Development, New Delhi
Fellow, Orfalea Center for Global and International Studies
University of California, Santa Barbara

Networking Workshop
Delhi Workshop (Co-convenor)

Ranjana Mukhopadhyaya
Associate Professor of East Asia Studies
University of Delhi
Delhi Workshop

Paul J. Nelson
Division Director of International Development
Graduate School of Public and International Affairs
University of Pittsburgh
Planning Workshop
Networking Workshop

Philip Oldenburg
Associate Director, South Asia Institute
Professor of Political Science
Columbia University, New York
Networking Workshop
South and Southeast Asia Workshop

Jacob Olupona
Professor of African and African American Studies
Harvard University
Africa and the Middle East Workshop

Atalia Omer
Assistant Professor of Religion, Conflict and Peace Studies
Kroc Institute for International Peace Studies
University of Notre Dame
Networking Workshop

David A. Palmer
Associate Professor of Sociology
University of Hong Kong
Shanghai Workshop

Ankur Patel
Program Officer, BAPS Chairities

New York and India
Planning Workshop

Marie Juul Petersen
Doctoral Student, Institute for Regional and Cross-Cultural Studies
University of Copenhagen, Denmark
Planning Workshop

Daniel Philpott
Associate Professor of Political Science
Joan B. Kroc Institute for Peace Studies
University of Notre Dame
Planning Workshop

Jan Nederveen Pieterse
Mellichamp Professor of Global Studies and Sociology
University of California, Santa Barbara
Networking Workshop

Lingam Raja
Associate Professor, Adult Continuing Education and Extension
Gandhigram Rural University
Tamil Nadu, India
Delhi Workshop

I. A. Rehman
Founding Member, Pakistan-India Human Rights Commission
Delhi Workshop

Victoria Riskin
Founder, Southern California Committee
Board Member, Human Rights Watch
Planning Workshop
Networking Workshop
Latin America and the Caribbean Workshop
South and Southeast Asia Workshop

Rowena Robinson
Professor, Center for the Study of Social Systems,
Jawaharlal Nehru University, New Delhi
Delhi Workshop

Wade Clark Roof
Professor of Religious Studies
University of California, Santa Barbara
Networking Workshop

Mona Kanwal Sheikh
Research Scholar, Danish Institute for International Studies, Copenhagen
and Orfalea Center for Global and International Studies
University of California, Santa Barbara
Planning Workshop
Networking Workshop

Ria Shibata
Graduate Student in Global Studies
Sophia University, Tokyo
South and Southeast Asia Workshop

Leonor Slavsky
Senior Researcher, National Institute of Anthropology
National Culture Secretariat, Argentina
Buenos Aires Workshop

Natalia L. Smakotina
Professor, Faculty of Global Processes
Lomonosov Moscow State University
Moscow Workshop

Siti Syamsiyatun
Director, Indonesian Consortium for Religious Studies (ICRS-Yogya)
Gadjah Mada University, Yogyakarta, Indonesia
Shanghai Workshop

Tadaatsu Tajima
Dean of College of Liberal Arts and Science
Tenshi College, Japan
Shanghai Workshop

Aaron Hahn Tapper
Founder and Co-Executive Director, Abraham's Vision
Assistant Professor of Theology and Religious Studies

University of San Francisco
Planning Workshop

Manindra Thakur
Associate Professor, Center for Political Studies
Jawaharlal Nehru University. New Delhi
Delhi Workshop

Thomas Tighe
CEO, Direct Relief International
Santa Barbara, California
Planning Workshop
Networking Workshop
Latin America and the Caribbean Workshop
Africa and the Middle East Workshop

Rebecca Tinsley
Director, Waging Peace
Planning Workshop

Idris A. Tsechoev
Deputy Provost, Lomonosov Moscow State University
Moscow Workshop

J. P. S. Uberoi
Professor of Sociology, Emeritus
Delhi School of Economics
University of Delhi
Delhi Workshop

Thomas Uthup
Research and Education Manager, United Nations Alliance of Civilizations, New York
South and Southeast Asia Workshop

Jonathan VanAntwerpen
Program Officer and Research Fellow, Social Science Research Council, New York
Planning Workshop

Toby Volkman
Director of Policy Initiatives and Secretary

The Henry Luce Foundation
Latin America and The Caribbean Workshop

James Wellman
Associate Professor
Jackson School of International Studies
University of Washington
Networking Workshop
Latin America and The Caribbean Workshop

Mark Woodward
Associate Professor of Religious Studies
Arizona State University
South and Southeast Asia Workshop

Surichai Wun'gaeo
Professor of Sociology
Director, Center for Peace and Conflict Studies
Chulalongkorn University
Bangkok, Thailand
South and Southeast Asia Workshop

Zhuo Xinping
Member of the Chinese Academy of Social Sciences
Member of the Degree Committee of Beijing Municipality
Member of the Academic Committee of the Institute for the Study of Buddhism
and Religious Theories at Renmin University
Adjunct Professor at Tsinghua University and Central University for Nationalities
Consultant

Xu Yihua
Professor, Center for American Studies and Department of International
Politics
Fudan University, China
Shanghai Workshop

Fr. Mikhail Zakharov
Archpriest, Russian Orthodox Church
Deputy Director of the Institute for Religious and Social Studies
Russian Academy of Science
Moscow Workshop

Hind Ahmed Zaki
Egyptian Political Organizer, Cairo
Cairo 2 Workshop

Karel Zelenka
Former Director, Catholic Relief Services, Haiti
Director, Catholic Relief Services, South Africa
Latin America and the Caribbean Workshop (Contributor)
Africa and the Middle East Workshop

Zhang Zhigang
Professor of Religious Studies
Beijing University, China
Shanghai Workshop

Mary Zurbuchen
Director, Asia and Russia Programs
Ford Foundation International Fellowships Program
New York
South and Southeast Asia Workshop

INDEX

States, 59; as related to globalization, 60; influence on politics, 47; in relation to humanitarian aid, 107
religious identity, 18, 32, 65–66, 68–69, 71, 73, 116
religious nationalism, 10, 20–21, 55; in India, 19; in Southeast Asia, 61
Robertson, Pat, 43, 67, 121n1; view on Islam, 59
Russia, 2, 17, 23, 27, 29, 66, 79, 86; homosexuality in, 95–100; nationalism in, 57–58; religion in, 57–59

Santa Barbara, 2, 15, 77–79, 95, 103
Saudi Arabia, 62, 103, 126n18; religious influence on politics in, 47; view on the Universal Declaration of Human Rights, 104
secularism, 2, 6, 9–10, 76, 78–79, 120n1; in Bangladesh, 7; in Egypt, 9, 72; in India, 7, 9, 19; in Iran, 9; in Pakistan, 7; in the Philippines, 71–72; in Turkey, 9; concept of, 5; meaning of, 6–7
secularization. *See* secularism.
secular nationalism, 7, 10, 18, 20, 23, 28, 30. *See also* nationalism

Shanghai, 12*fig.;* workshop in, 2, 14, 61, 68–69, 71, 86
Shanghai University, 2, 13–14
Syria, 17, 24, 66; extremist rebel movement in, 46

Tahrir Square, xiv*fig.,* 1, 53, 112*fig.,* 113, 115
Taliban, 18–19; definition of, 109
Taksim Square: protests in, 4, 114
televangelist, 43, 46, 67, 116: in the Middle East, 43–45; in the United States, 59
terrorism, 15, 120n5; in Iraq, 108; in Japan, 40; relation to religion, 30. *See also* religious extremism
Tibet, 27, 88, 99, 125n8
Turkey, 9, 67; protests in, 4, 114–15

Ukraine, 27, 113, 118; protests in, 26, 114
UN. *See* United Nations
UNAMI. *See* United Nations Assistance for Iraq
United Nations, 35, 82, 104–5, 126n17; creation of, 29; role in Iraq invasion, 107–8
United Nations Assistance for Iraq, 108
universal human rights. *See* human rights